GLEANINGS REVISITED

NOSTALGIC THOUGHTS OF A BEDFORDSHIRE FARMER'S BOY

E. W. O'Dell

The
Book
Castle

SKETCH MAP OF OLD BARTON

(Not to Scale)

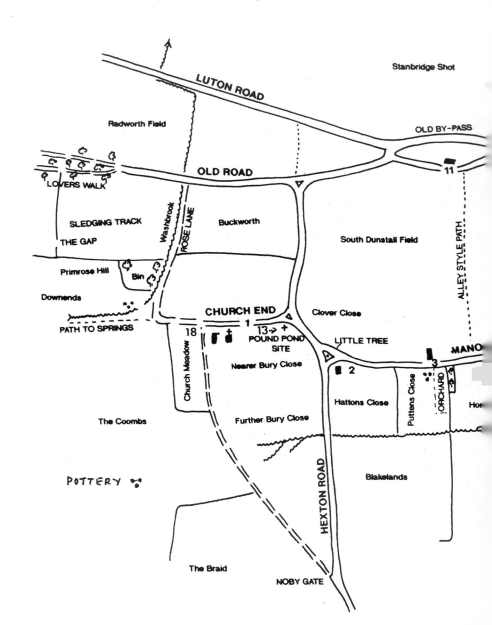

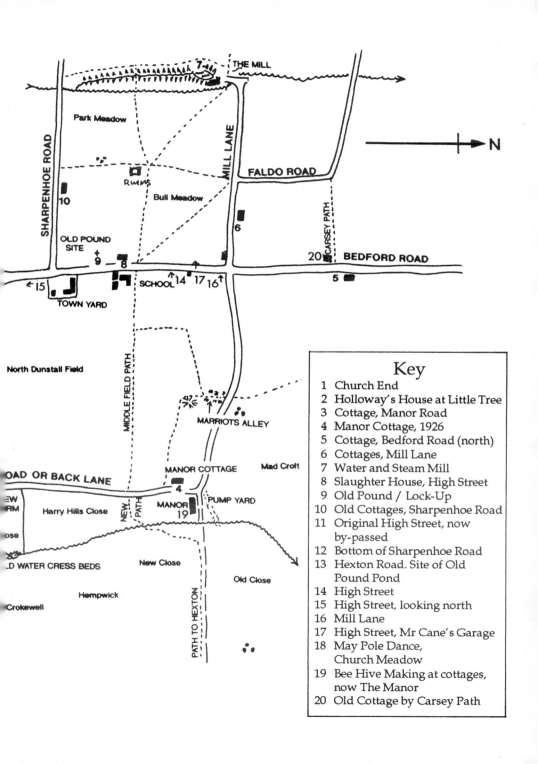

This revised and expanded edition published August 1995
by
The Book Castle
12 Church Street
Dunstable
Bedfordshire LU5 1RU

Original edition published privately 1976

ISBN 1 871199 77 8

Computer typeset by Keyword, Aldbury, Hertfordshire.
Printed by Progressive Printing (UK) Ltd., Leigh-on-Sea, Essex.

Foreword

Change has never been more rapid in rural areas than in the last few decades, from the early nineteen-twenties onwards. For example, scythes were first replaced by reapers, or as we called them, binders, then came the huge combine harvesters, all between my childhood and manhood. For children now it can never be quite the same as in those days when fun and games were combined with a strict upbringing. My imagination slips back frequently and I try to relive for a few seconds those figmentations, sucking them like sweets for as long as they can be made to last. Many dim and run away, never to return, like raindrops running down a window pane.

Steeped in nostalgia, some of these thoughts I write here, before they fade for ever, are perhaps for posterity. They may not be absolutely accurate in every way, but are as near as I can get at this time. No longer available, a shorter version of these

Bedford Road (north).

memoirs was published in booklet form in 1976, and I am pleased to be able to meet continuing demand with this fuller edition. I must stress that in this book are written my own personal thoughts, and I hope I offend no-one.

The village of Barton-in-the-Clay has changed out of all recognition and will continue to do so, for people must have homes to live in. The Green Belt, unfortunately being made of elastic, is stretched into an incurable disease of urban spread. It would seem a small piece of the old village disappears almost imperceptibly every year. Only a few of the older houses remain, and still fewer old villagers, but the hills are still there, the Chiltern escarpment south of the village being steadily encroached by nut hazel and whitethorn. But still they pour out

their clear streams, one either side of the village, as when they once served the less fortunate who had no wells for drinking or washing water. The menfolk no longer carry water on yokes, as the village is now on the mains, of course. The flowers still bloom on the hills, and birds build nests; the bright-eyed squirrel and the soft-voiced dove are at home there. My niece who is a Lakeland lass refers to the Barton Hills as bumps, but to me they have a Lilliputian charm and I will refer to them constantly in later pages.

Here lived a man
Who wrote and tried
But never was
   quite versified.

Rosebay Willow Herb

Family

My earliest recollections are of my father; he was always there somewhere, dressed (apart from Sundays and special occasions) as I can see him now in breeches, leggings and heavy boots, his boots hand-made by Lawsons of Luton, iron-heeled and heavily studded. They lasted many years, and, through constant splashing whilst milking his cows, became hard and encrusted with a layer of solidified milk. They eventually became unbendable, as, I might add, he became that way himself in later years. However, he reckoned the boots he wore were comfortable and at least moulded and beaten to fit the shape of his toes, which had after many years been kicked and trodden on by various animals into unnatural shapes. I can remember him easing them off in the evening, after perhaps ploughing all day, with a sigh of relief.

I would mostly be in bed when he came home, but would try to keep awake until I heard his heavy boots tramping up the cobbled path. I somehow felt secure once I knew he was home, and the house would finally fill with peace, any nervous thoughts I may have had quickly dispelled so that I slept instantly. When memories drift back to the old days, of course my father was always there, for a family was a unit and most time was spent with the family. If I didn't happen to be with them for an hour or two, chances were he soon knew where I was and woe betide me if I had misbehaved in any way. Parents in those days had a grapevine unsurpassed, and strictness, thank goodness, was so much more severe.

Father was a God-fearing man who had his own pew in Chapel, was quick-witted, rather sarcastic, hard working and dogmatic, quite a remarkable man, and if cornered in any verbal argument would back out of the conversation with his pet quote, 'Ah, well, I shan't say anything', and opt out before he could be proved in any way wrong.

I being the youngest of three, having an older brother and sister, do not remember my Mother at all, she having died when I was three months old. My Father married again, my Step-mother taking much on; she must have had a heart of gold through this did not show very much to us, being very strict. I suppose through having taken so much on it was not until later years that she really showed us any kindness and as she mellowed into old age, we got on very well and could then do nothing wrong. Three children, a smallholding, a few cows and a vegetable round in Luton where my Father 'hawked' every Saturday morning, this was not much for any woman to run after, but Mother managed very well, keeping us fed and even if not very smart at least clean. Her cooking, however, left much to be desired, apart from Yorkshire pudds and beef pudding, at which she really excelled. One thing I hated was cold Yorkshire pudding; unfortunately it was a standby. Mother would serve it in many different ways, one being with jam, cold. This used to give me a revolting feeling and would perhaps be served several days until I finally gave in and ate it. I still feel ill even now just thinking about it.

A great one for hoarding was Mother. When I was about five or six years old, our front room (which was really at the back) was kept open for Sundays and High days, such as visitors at Christmas, when the family would always meet. The table opened up to seven feet in length, and we would bring out the Spinning Jenny as we wrongly called it, a sort of revolving arrow made from Meccano. Each of us took a spin, and if the arrow rested on a piece of chocolate, sweet or sugar mouse, it was yours; home made wine and sherry for the grown ups and ginger beer for the children. We were allowed to stay up late and had a good time.

Over the years the front room began to fill up and took a great deal to clean out (even for Christmas). Even this became impossible eventually and made Father rant on a bit. The whole room steadily became cluttered, and only a strip mat from the living room door to the stair door in the opposite corner remained negotiable. It was always something of a mystery what the large cardboard boxes and sundry other items contained, for we were never allowed to look into things, and it was taboo for us to even look in the cupboards. Every door had its own squeak, and Mother could hear us from any part of the house and would shot, 'What are you doing in that cupboard?' Much of the floor space was taken up with milk, cans, jugs and large flat containers used to skim off the maximum amount of cream for butter making, a ritual that Father had for about twenty minutes every week. Sitting by the fire, the churn clasped between his knees, he would churn away without stopping, for if one stopped, it 'went back' they said.

A great hoard of junk was collected throughout the ensuing years; nothing thrown away, the bedrooms and little cupboards in the alcove were soon filled and sealed with bric-à-brac, never to be opened. In the large barn at the south end the mangle and coal were kept. The small diamond window was soon covered with ivy and cobwebs, it became darker each year, soon one could get at the coal only. We did have a few white mice but they escaped, never to be seen again. I rather suspect they were devoured by the field mice which took over, their whereabouts only known by the droppings on the front of the cupboard shelves. Food was then moved to the front room, thus creating more havoc and requiring painstaking steps to find the required article.

Mother had a rat or two during the winter months which could be heard scampering under the roof or gnawing at some cupboard partition during the quiet of the evenings. It was something for Mother to fall back on, anything missing or lost was blamed onto the rat and easily explained away. We also had a bees' nest above the ceiling in the centre of the room, between ceiling and bedroom floor. The bees entering from the outside would make a large dark stain each summer, clearly visible as the honey accumulated.

Forthcoming events were foretold with explicit faith, Mother being a regular reader of 'Old Moore's Almanack'. Any national disaster and Mother would say 'I told you so', with a smile and a nod of the head. One thing Mother always failed at, an oven. Wherever we lived she could never get an oven to go, I think because she would never use enough coal. She always finished up using small paraffin stoves that stood over much of the kitchen floor and were of course alarmingly dangerous. I remember 'G' purchased half a dozen turkey chicks with a foster mother hen. We let them stroll round the meadow in the wet grass until only one remained for Christmas. This was to be a great treat, our first ever turkey. Needless to say the oven wouldn't go – so we had sausage and mash for Christmas dinner. 'G' gave the oven to his worker and some time later I saw it installed in his house looking resplendent, shining and polished; they thought it a wonderful thing.

One cannot think back without recalling the outside privy, which was an integral part of our lives. This was a worm-eaten double seater with an inch piece missing from the rear, uncomfortable for anyone reaching that far, for only having one bucket, the smaller hole was covered with a box containing torn newspapers and magazines. The ivy encroached the wooden sides, so one sat in semi-darkness, with ivy and cobwebs, and an occasional beautiful moth would be seen in trembling flight. One could sit in restful serenity and read if the light was good enough, or just sit and meditate according to mood. No visitor solved the intricacy of shutting the door, being too short of time.

> 'Is it true', said the crow,
> 'I'm the ugliest bird you know?'

I well remember a rather funny episode concerning our outside privy. A lovely cat which befriended us remained semi-wild and always had her kittens several hundred yards away in an old 'moggy' tree, only bringing them home when they were two or three months old. Then, of course, never having seen anyone in their lives, they were wild. She always brought them home to the privy under the seat, where they would spit and curse in an alarming manner once anyone was enthroned. On one occasion we had a young lady, a friend of the family, staying with us, who was very quietly spoken, sedate, and very prim. On this memorable occasion on-one had warned her about the cats being in residence. She went for her quiet meditation, only to return very ruffled, ashen-faced and more or less in blind terror. She had of course taken down her bloomers and was just lowering herself peacefully when all hell broke loose, much to the hilarity of us children, who could not suppress our obvious mirth. We, unlike the cats, looked on the funny side of all this, of course.

Like most children we had our arguments but they never had to last long. I, being the youngest, had to sit within arm's reach of Father and often had punishment meted out to me which the others should have had. On the low elm beam which stretched from one end of the room to the other was placed, rather handily just above his rocking chair, a nice hazel stick. He didn't often use this, for a glance upwards usually sufficed.

Between us we concocted nicknames for Father and both of our uncles. The uncle who lived just up the lane (the lane was really Manor Road, but everyone called it Back Lane at that time) had been in the fourteen-eighteen war as a Sergeant, and was indeed still very strict. If any of us aggravated him, his face

Three brothers, from left to right, Charles, George and William.

5

would redden up and his lush moustache would grow visibly whiter; in fact he looked the part, so behind his back we called him 'Sarge'. For all that he was a very lovable uncle and a great gardener.

The other uncle, a tailor from Eastbourne, used to visit us regularly, staying to help with harvest. He was a great Methodist and knew all the hymns and tunes off by heart; him we christened, perhaps somewhat unkindly, Levi. On Sunday evenings, much to the anguish of us children, he would perform on the piano, and we were expected to join in, going through the hymn books singing his favourite tunes, and with his somewhat ill-fitting teeth and a voice peculiar to say the least, would keep us in suppressed mirth. Any sign of a giggle would probably mean early bed; to laugh at the wrong time was bad enough, but to laugh when religious subjects were being expounded would have meant almost death to us.

Last but not least was Father, who for the want of a better name we called 'G', his christian name being George. I shall refer to him by his nickname for the rest of the book. Times were hard in the mid-twenties, our food was often subsidised by food off the farm, the odd rabbit or hare, and if we were very lucky a pheasant could find its way mysteriously into the pantry. I have known him shoot lapwings from the bedroom window, and send me scurrying out for them. During mealtimes 'G' often had a doze in between first and second courses – I imagine this started as a form of protest and finished up a habit. 'G' used to tell me about the time he caught two hares in one snare, one being caught the ordinary way, the other being inquisitive by nature had its legs caught up in the wire, so trapping the two together. Rabbits were caught in cruel gin traps in those days, and one heard of sparrow pies being eaten.

Aunt Sally looked after me as my Mother died when I was three months old, and was always my favourite. If it rained when I first started school, I used to go down to Clipstone Cottages where she lived, for dinner; I didn't need much of an excuse. Incidentally my sister Rene remembers that all the

6

people living at Clipstone Cottages used to hang their frying pans upside down on the back wall of their houses. The fat, dripping down the bricks, hung like stalactites underneath each pan.

Aunt Sally did inadvertently give me a cruel shock when my Uncle died, as she insisted that I should go up and see him in his coffin – which was the done thing in those days. I remember so well after all these years, sitting downstairs waiting in a room, the lace curtains making the room seem dark; shell fragments stood on the wicker table, remnants of the 1918 war, a large green-leafed aspidistra in the window, the rolled Union Jack half-covered behind the curtain on the door, two handsome pictures on the wall, of women in long blue robes clinging desperately to huge wooden crosses half-submerged in seething sea and rocks. In the distance the Harlington trains could be heard, as I was called unwillingly upstairs and there in the coffin lay poor Uncle, his face the only remains of his identity, and the smell of death. It took me years to forget; I had to put my hand gently on his cold forehead. I crept terrified down the twisted stairs.

Father at Work

Every Saturday morning 'G' used to hawk vegetables round Luton. Many he grew himself, and eggs he would supplement by collecting them from various parts of the village. Rabbits could always be sold, and he kept his poker under the trolley seat in readiness for when the horse walked slowly up the Barton cutting; he would often knock a rabbit off that was feeding. The poor thing would roll down the cut almost into his hands, and he could skin it in a few minutes and sell it for tenpence (old money). Every week a rabbit skin man came round the village and 'G' had them hanging outside the back door, drying, in readiness. The princely sum of one penny was given for a good skin.

We had an off-white oilcloth on the table for practical

Barton Cutting, 1900.

purposes which years later amused my wife. 'G' had skinned a rabbit, leaving on the head, which was considered a choice portion, and as kids we used to argue over whose turn it was to have it, being quite a delicacy. One rabbit 'G' had thrown on the cloth must have been there some time for it left an indelible print on the cloth, which always reminded me of the 'Turin Shroud'.

In the winter months it was very cold sitting on the front of the trolley, my short legs kicking off the G. O'Dell & Sons emblazoned across the front. Often I would hang on the rear of the trolley and run for long distances to keep warm. One could see small pieces of brushwood sticking out of the short corn. 'G' said this was to stop poachers netting partridges. He would keep his eyes under the telephone wires, which festoon the roadside, on which incidentally were placed corks, so the flying birds could see the wires more easily. One could often pick up a partridge which had been killed this way. Once out of the top of the cutting, he would tell me of the time he worked in the fields, often starting at 5.30 in the morning if he was at bean or clover cart, as the crops had to be carted while the dew was on them to stop shelling out. He received ten shillings a week for this and had to walk the two miles and get there on time. However, he was offered a more lucrative job on another farm for ten shillings and sixpence a week which he took, and because he didn't give the customary notice, was taken to Court. His fine was ten shillings. Someone told Grandpa outside the Court he could appeal, as he was a minor (under fourteen). Grandpa said, 'Shan't bother, it will be throwing good money after bad', so poor old 'G' had to work twenty weeks with his extra tanner to pay off the fine.

Sometime after, he worked in the hat trade in Luton and had to walk the six miles and get there in time for seven-thirty. The other men lived in Luton but 'G' being the best timekeeper had the key to the factory. 'G' often told the tale of a man who was a notoriously fast walker who, coming out of the Streatley turn at the top of the cutting, with four and a half miles to walk to Luton, on being met with a cart going the same way, was asked if he wanted a lift. 'No thanks', came the reply, 'ain't got time'.

Sharpenhoe Road, looking east.

Apart from the land 'G' farmed on the holding, he had many other pieces. Some were down Sharpenhoe Road, and to the left of the brook, a field called 'Lie Piece' where the old Coprolite mining was done in the eighties. These Coprolite nodes were a dark hard fossil purported to be the remains of prehistoric animals' excrement and mollusc casts and then of course solidified. The beds lay patchily through Barton and Shillington to Cambridge and were worked in the eighteenth century; trenches were dug up to twenty feet deep to obtain these nodules, which were washed in slurry pits to clean them. Hundreds were employed on the working and the population rose about that time.

Clipstone Cottages were built at that time also. I was told my Grandfather had an arm broken during a cave-in. I sent a sample to 'Lawes' who said they were extremely hard and high in phosphates and would take a considerable amount of grinding. The analysis of 27.8% P_2O_5 is of interest, this figure compares with about 34% P_2O_5 for the rock phosphate which is imported from North Africa. Most of the meadows at the end of Mill Lane he also rented. These included sheds at the mill which he used for many years as a cow house. In the west wall of the shed still remained bricks from a house where he lived as a child. Other land was up Old Road, by Mount Pleasant, which was owned by Barton Lime Works. This made a rough and exciting ride home down deep ruts formed by the rains. A scotch had to be placed under the wheels to skid down, and the horse had to sit well back in the breeching to hold back the load.

Holloway's House at Little Tree.

We are very shy, said the pheasant
I fear our flesh is far too pleasant.

I can still remember the mill wheel turning, for there was plenty of water in those days. I watched the great overshoot wheel turn slowly and splash white cascades of water over, and the water from the head at the back had an overspill. Water would gush down after heavy rain over a series of falls to stop the bank being washed away. Much work must have been done to raise the brook and the mill head to such a height. 'G' told me how a man had once hung himself down there, and he was one of these who had to cut him down, in the darkness. With the steady drip of water over the wheel, it made a very eerie situation indeed. The only kingfisher I ever saw at Barton was down at the mill, darting over the water, its streaking sapphire blue against the dark of the crack willows. Brown trout swam up the stream, and would lie under the bridges. 'G' would sometimes catch one with his hands or a bucket. In later years I have shot them with a four-ten gun. A few smaller trout managed to reach the Washbrook Meadow at the foot of the hills where their life expectancy was even shorter. What sheer delight to 'G', with parched young throat, on a flat stone or slab to drink straight from the hill, to drink wondrously cold water originating from the hill springs.

Barton Water and Steam Mill.

Now the grey wheel stands there silent,
Save the echoed drip by night,
When the great moon lifts above her,
Piercing in a ghostly white.

Schooldays and Sundays

From Manor Road, (or Back Lane as it was then called), we would walk up the Main Street to school. In about 1927 there were very few cars and they travelled very slowly. The drivers would shout at us to get out of the way and I vividly recall one incident when a driver stopped his car and waved a horse whip at us, threatening to give us the hiding of our lives. There used to be a toll bridge at one time at the brook south of 'Speed the Plough Inn'; a row of cottages north of the stream were inhabited by the Clarks and Barons. Bensons lived in a single house south of the stream. It is most likely that some of the drivers, rather than pay the toll, would cut off across the field, down 'Markets Lane' and over towards Faldo Road, down the row ploughed, out onto Grindstone Lane.

One of the first things I remember at school was drawing in little boxes filled with a light coloured sand, and trying to print

Slaughter House, High Street.

with slate pencils on a slate; the noise put one's teeth on edge and I have wondered since if the teacher had any, but perhaps this was unfair. From the front playground one could see what was taking place on the main road. We used to keep watch for the cattle drivers; perhaps a hundred or more cattle would come charging through the village on their way to one of the markets, as a rule with only two professional drovers; how they ever coped I will never know. The cattle hardly ever stopped running and it was more like a Wild West drive than anything else, and the verges suffered accordingly, at any rate, they never looked the same afterwards for a while. To the suppressed mirth of the class, a girl stood up and asked teacher why some of the cattle tried to ride on each other's backs!

High Street.

Vagabonds or tramps would reach the village after walking from Luton at about the same time every weekday, a sad array of dejected men and assortments of rags, bundles and tea cans, long flowing beards covering most of their faces. Mothers would grab their children and cross the road; children on their own would hide frightened. Today, youths through fashion are not dissimilar in appearance, especially the youths of both sexes who walk around in things called 'jeans' with a jacket to match. In my day only engine drivers, thrashing and ploughing

14

engine men dressed thus and they took them off as soon as they were home, for they would not dare to be seen out in such apparel. In these days of decadence and unbeautification, one has to tear out the knees of trousers to look 'with it', wear dark glasses as though blind, and the latest – men tying their hair at the back of the head, which reminds me of the arse end of a horse. Tailors' names were once discreetly placed on the inside jacket pocket, but are now blazoned with other nonsensical names in prominent colours positioned on the clothing.

My scholastic efforts were short lived. It was evident at an early stage that my academic career would be very short indeed, and the headmaster soon sensed the futility of further attempts to instil a modicum of learning in me. So, making the best of a bad job, he sent me along with one or two others of equally low intelligence into his rather over-large garden, replacing pen with spade, or fighting a losing battle mowing about a quarter of an acre of orchard with a nine inch hand mower. As autumn neared, the mower had a distinct tendency to run towards the William peartree. We were told we could have a few 'fallers' as long as we didn't interfere with those on the trees. The telltale cudgels* hanging in the tree were ample evidence that we were running true to form.

One of my earliest recollections at school – we started at three years old in those days – was a special treat, being called into the room with the biguns* to hear my first gramophone. I remember still sitting puzzled as the music scratched, staring at the huge horn-like speaker. I thought there must have been human bones or something inside the box; being a little stupid I voiced my thoughts, much to the amusement of my sister Irene.

As infants we watched the old biplanes battle their way over the playground. We always waved and shouted 'drop us a penny, mate' and from their open cockpits they would often wave to us as they passed slowly over, at about 65 m.p.h.

I never rose to the lofty heights of monitor, but I did make chief stoker, going round the huge fires in the class rooms and making them up with coal. The ones who sat near them were almost roasted out, but the ones at the rear had a much rougher time during the coldest weather.

Empire Day, 24th May, open day at school, boys and girls – mostly the girls – would bedeck themselves with daisy chains and waving flags, would sing patriotic songs about 'Britons never being slaves', etc. My Aunt Sally had a large Union Jack on a bamboo pole, which was always in demand owing to its size. This I would borrow yearly, for though my singing left much to be desired, my flag waving had to be seen to be appreciated.

A very jolly Rev. J. Spokes used to visit the school. His hand would go into his pocket and as quick as lightening he would throw a handful of sweets on the ground. There was then one mad rush and if you could pick one up before a studded boot was stamped on your hand, by an older boy, you were indeed lucky. There must have been some thought of turning the Manor School into a C. of E. I still remember 'G' saying 'On no account must you put C. of E. on the front of your exercise books'. This of course brought me a lot of trouble from the Headmaster.

The boys' outdoor urinals were separated, the younger from the older, by a six foot wall. This did not, however, deter the older ones who could, with a certain manipulation, squirt over the top onto the less fortunate 'little'uns', who in their turn after changing playgrounds gave their own back.

From the boys' outside 'loo' one could climb over the bicycle shed, where rows of trap doors housed the buckets for the girls. The favourite trick was to open these doors carefully to observe the rows of bottoms hanging down, like large white plums. They soon twigged this, due I think to the inrush of cold air round their posteriors. This adventure came to a sudden end when one enterprising youth inserted his gloved hand, which unfortunately held a bunch of stinging nettles.

My school reports were not impressive and did nothing to make 'G' glad he had a son still at school, and to make matters worse, a few years previously my cousin Ivan had started at Barton School, then on to Bedford Modern and passed for Cambridge, which in those days especially was something really exceptional.

We lived a busy but happy life, though work could become

a drudgery. Thinking back, my head was either patted of banged. The pats were less frequent than the bangs, and I must have walked about permanently concussed. This would at least account for 'walking about in a dream' as I was frequently told.

✦ ✦ ✦ ✦ ✦

Both my sister and I had to attend Chapel at least twice on Sundays, and I rather suspect it was a relief for her to get away from the drudgery of house work for a while, for she, like myself, had little time for play. Anniversary came once a year; we had to stand and perform in front of a packed house, singing praises of various sorts, clad in our Sunday best new suits, and the girls would have new dresses, usually pinafore dresses, starched and white, the little shoulder frills sticking out as though their angel wings were already on the way, laced boots almost up to the knees, which are now fashionable again, looking just as ugly as they did then.

Later we were promoted to the choir, not for our voices but because lanky boys and girls of fifteen and sixteen would hardly look right standing with the children. We stood up in the choir in full view, and our apprehension must have been shared by the choirmaster, Mr Frank Carter. He would raise his baton, up we would stand with very little room, the smallest would try to hide behind the more corpulent elders, holding our music sheets which some of us couldn't read. Some had good voices, some mediocre, others, myself included, more raucous than sweet. What a thankless task our choirmaster must have had; it would have been easier to try and make seagulls sing! When we were young, relatives would visit Barton on Anniversary Day, have tea and go to Chapel. Afterwards we would meet our parents and go for a walk, perhaps up the hills of Church End, and I would think back to the Scottish sword dancers I once saw there. Passing the Church we would soon be in open fields, called the Coombs (an old word meaning valley), following the twisting stream that glistened in places through the thick hedgerow, topped with travellers joy or old man's beard, by the nut hazels up to the springs themselves. Perhaps this is as far as we would go, and if given the chance would join boys trying to kick a ball up White Hill, a hill which is completely covered with scrub and trees today. We would scamper around Plum Pudding Hill, our feet echoing on the chalk, making a hollow sound. We would imagine all the hill hollow, where little people lived. Who was it said they came out only in the first light of the day when the grasses opened to release their water vapour; in this dew they would wash, the men wore hats of acorn cups, the ladies bonnets of upturned violets of blue and white, with floral skirts of dog daisies, tied with spiders' gossamer? They were said only to come out when the anemone pulsatilla (pasque flower) was in bloom, for this was the flower they were said to have lived on, this was why the flower was so rare. At the first sign of day, when the first rabbit clawed down to self interment, they too clambered down to their cathedral – like caverns, built in the chalk, lit only by the holes of worms running up to the outside world. We would catch water from the springs, throwing out their clear water from holes in the hillside.

Plum Pudding Hill.

Dreams that flood as a tide by night,
In a woodland hood of branches flow,
Twisting brambles writhe for light,
They sink in the damp moss deep below.

For dreamers dream in their pink warm sheets,
Brows are puckered in a frown,
The soul flies high when the dream's complete,
Then arching, drifting down.

✦ ✦ ✦ ✦ ✦

EXTRACT FROM PARISH MAGAZINE, 1898.
ANNUAL SCHOOL FEAST
RECTORY MEADOW

Proceedings commenced with a merry peal of Bells from Belfrey Tower; then came the enlivening strains of Gravenhurst Brass Band which played throughout the afternoon. Scrambles, Races and various sports followed. Amongst these pastimes the Maypole dance showed pre-eminently as the event of the afternoon. Some twenty-five girls

May Pole Dancing, Rectory Meadow.

19

draped all in white and crowned with wreaths of various blossoms went through a series of intricate figures by which means they plaited the pole with ribbons of many hues; this spectacle, beautiful in itself, was greatly enhanced by its surroundings, the performance taking place on a natural plateau close to the Rectory Mount which was gaily fringed with rich clusters of golden iris.

This season ninety children from London have been sent to Barton by the children's 'Fresh Air Mission' for a fortnight each; many thanks to those who kindly lodged and catered for them.

✦ ✦ ✦ ✦ ✦

When work finished on Sunday mornings, the orchard became a sort of meeting place of 'G's' friends, where they would chat and stand looking over the doors at pigs and talk of general events, and run down neighbours and themselves. 'G' believed in only doing the absolutely necessary on the Sabbath and used to say harvest was never spoilt by leaving it in the field on Sunday. He used to solemnize this by forbidding us to play any sort of games; his wish was easily achieved, for after going to Chapel perhaps three times in one day, there was little time left, and one daren't go against his wish dressed in Sunday best. Dressed thus we would often visit Aunts and Uncles, where we were asked in, given a chair, and if our parents were present, would have to sit there without fidgeting in disciplined silence for what seemed to us eternity, for not to be well behaved was, and is, about the very worst kind of self incrimination, and let down for your parents, that one could inflict.

How things change! In early days the Sunday morning was so quiet one could hear the sheep bells on the hills. I have never heard anything to approach this pleasantry on the Sabbath. Nowadays it's the steady banging of the clay pigeon shooters, or someone inconsiderately starting up a rotavator or a powered lawn mower. However light the evenings and long now, these powered strimmers, which make a fiendish noise, should be banned on Sundays. These machines seem noisier in the evening, when all else is quiet.

Clay hard is my water bed,
Smooth washed are my flints
Wood anemone, horse tail,
Fragrant wild mints.
Strange men from the hill forts,
Bowls that were clayed
In pleasantries of summer,
Their children here played.

After our walk on the hills it would be time for bed, as it was school in the morning, and 'G' would always quote, if only to annoy –

Early to bed, early to rise,
Makes a young man
Healthy and wise.

If one had a few playthings our Mother would sing:

Pack up your troubles in your old kit bag
And smile boys, that's the style.

This never ceased to annoy me and I would never raise the required smile, but could be up the stairs, Mother holding the candle, and with a short prayer 'Gentle Jesus, meek and mild' then be tucked in for the night, not to be heard till morning.

Fun and Games

One had to hurry home from school and milk at least a little from the easy cows to help out, and then put them out by the side of the road to graze for an hour or two. Sometimes this was done in Mill Lane, and often over to Back Lane. This was not too bad a job providing one kept one's wits about one; the hardest part was to watch other children the same age playing games.

At certain slacker times one had a few nights off, when a variety of games were played. They seemed to be seasonal, coming round each year at the same time. No one was in charge of the changeover, but change they mysteriously did. Some of them I remember were skipping and hopscotch for the girls. The girls when skipping would sing a little song.

> My Mother said, I never should
> Play with the gypsies in the wood,
> If I did she would say
> Naughty girl to disobey.

(Then skipping faster all the time)

> Salt, mustard, vinegar, pepper,
> Lay the table, knives and forks,
> Bring me in a leg of pork.
> If it's lean, make it clean,
> If it's fat, take it back.

When the girls played hopscotch, the boys would run and kick the spitcher* away from the girls, but usually we were too involved with our own games – hoops, huntsmen and hounds. The hounds would set off along some dark hedgerow and after a reasonable start, the huntsmen would follow, their only clues being if the hounds yelped. If they didn't, then the huntsmen would shout 'If you don't holler, we shan't foller'. The hounds would then shout 'Yelp, yelp', and having some idea of their whereabouts the huntsmen would set off in hot pursuit. These runs would often go round the whole village, and would certainly drain off any surplus energy, and we would finish up gasping under one of the few street lights to discuss the chase.

Another popular game which reached its peak during the building of the council houses down Mill Lane was 'Ackies out'. I suppose half built houses were the ideal place for such a game. The game was played like this. One boy would close his eyes, with one foot on an old tin, and count up to a given number. The rest of the gang would hide from the counter, who would look for the others and try to touch them, but if they could race back to the tin and touch it with their feet first they were safe and could hide the next time. The one who was caught or touched had to do the hunting next time. The greatest thrill in this game was to race back and give the tin the hardest kick one could, and satisfactory results were obtained if the tin finished up over the hedge.

'Tippet' or 'Tipcat' was a game played with a stick and a piece of wood about five or six inches long, pointed at each end, which had to be thrown in a chalk circle, something like cricket, runs would be scored and the tippet could be struck near its pointed end and as it flew upwards could be clouted again. 'Dragons' we played too, one strong boy standing at the front, the other would bend down, grasping each other's thighs, while the others jumped on them, the underneath ones would move forward and shake and twist slowly trying to dislodge the ones on the top, when a great heap of twisting bodies would collapse laughing on the grass. As most boys had short trousers and woollen button-necked jumpers with long sleeves, they caused much amusement among themselves with their very stretched jumpers and sleeves hanging sometimes a foot below their hands. This did not go down very well with their parents!

Most of these games were played just in Mill Lane, for it was a lot wider owing to the cottages being built near enough to the road and on the same level, and before families lived there. With a piece of chalk, stumps were drawn on Mr Godfrey's barn for cricket, or sometimes for devilment the boys would tie two doors together by the knobs, knock the doors, then run and hide. One family would try to open the door, in doing so would rattle her neighbour's and they would try the same thing. If it was dusk, and it usually was, the husband would come round from

Cottages at Mill Lane.

the back and shout, 'Wait till I catch you little buggers', little knowing one of his children was more than likely a chief proponent of the escapade. Another trick was a long piece of cotton pinned to the window frame with a button threaded on to it. One would pull the thread so that the button would tap, tap, on the window, when they came out the cotton would be slackened so that nothing was seen.

For cricket we had stumps broken from the hedge and the bats were fashioned with a chopper at home. Soft balls were used usually, never busters.* Football too had its place, and more often than not the same balls were used. If anyone had a semblance of a full-sized football there would be a queue outside his house to borrow it. Goal posts were jackets on a stalm* cut from the hedgerow. 'G' would let us play in Bull Meadow as no cows were there, and later in the evening half the village boys from nine to thirty years of age would be playing, roughly half on each side. Of course none of us had football boots in those days, so that school boots had a fair scuffing. Forays down to the pond in early spring to reach out for frogspawn, where each frog laid thousands of eggs, each wrapped in balloons of jelly; these were taken home in jam jars where perhaps a few turned into frogs and would escape into the world.

A rare treat at the weekend would be a ride somewhere in the gig, where I would sit high up on the seat looking at the wondrous countryside. 'G' would often give the horse a flick with his whip. The horse then jerked forward and I would topple off the back if they didn't grab my knees. One memorable occasion I not only fell off the seat, but clean out of the back of the gig. My brother and sister dared not tell, then I had to run and catch up and jump in the back.

Springtime

The splash of gulls
    Behind the plough.
A robin sings
    On orchard bough.
Spring must be here.

Land sides
    And mould board gleams.
Children playing
    On the green.
Spring must be here.

The open fields
    With their winter's corn
Look greener now
    With every morn.
Spring must be here.

The yellow palm
    That's hanging now
With golden wands
    On every bough.
Spring must be here.

Church bells,
    The valley rings,
The lark above
    The sanfoin sings.
Spring must be here.

Brooks run high,
    Field drains sing,
Skylarks trill
    High on the wing.
Spring must be here.

The orange beak
    Of blackbirds glows,
Sings all the sweetest
    Songs he knows.
Spring must be here.

The blue and white
    Of violet beds
The aromatic fragrance
    Spreads.
Spring must be here.

The cowslips
    On the bankside bowed,
Hang their heads
    In yellow clouds.
Spring must be here.

The furry leveret
    From furrow lines,
Runs disturbed
    From shiny tines.
Spring must be here.

Moles are in the pasture
    With their daily toils,
Show when it is working,
    Pushing up the soil.
Spring must be here.

The squealing of
    The hungry pigs.
The rooks build
    Airy nests of twigs.
Spring must be here.

First signs of Spring, the white thorn shoots green speckles in the hedgerow; we used to nibble these, calling it 'Bread and Cheese'. The hemlock shoots, and by the damp water places celandines open up green gold cups, younger girls make mud

Violet.

pies and hide them in the tree roots to dry, the violets and wood anemones take their chance to bloom before the leafy canopies are too cool for the first bees. The deafening clamour of the dawn chorus is heard every morning, and the first tracks are made in the green banks, for it would be time for the birds to nest.

Safaris would be made searching for eggs, the rarer they were the farther we seemed to have to go. I was a hooked addict for nesting, no tree too difficult, no distance too far to walk. Every tree and hedgerow was explored with great thoroughness, even keepered woods were entered with great care and craft. I must add, though, that once an egg from any nest was obtained, a twicer would hardly ever be taken, unless on a rare occasion for a swop.

Forty years ago many of the birds were not on the protected list anyway, but there were, however, exceptions. Pigeons and moorhens were considered fair game for the frypan. 'G' always asked me to take all the sparrow eggs I could find, so I used to visit their nests regularly, a sort of egg collection, from thatch and trees and buildings, for if the young hatched they were taken to the soft milky wheat fields where they wasted more than they ate. I still feel an irresistible urge to look into the newly made nests of a thrush, and in the still damp dark bowl of the nest, fashioned with its breast, see the beautiful blue spotted eggs clustered like precious stones cupped deep in two hands. The only thing to compete is the song of the bird itself.

> Up in the high woods
> I heard call
> A piping songthrush
> Lovesong fall
> Through early mist
> The soft notes float
> What a great voice
> From such a small throat.

Legs were stung in the young nettles, boots wet through and clothes many times torn. 'G' then at the end of his patience and with more than a little prompting from Mother, threatened me with a good hiding the very next time he heard that I had climbed a tree, and what 'G' said he meant, being a man of his word. Of course before long the inevitable happened. Having been told on good authority of a brown owl's nest in a moggy* tree at the eastern end of Park Meadow, I fought against it all day to no avail. I could almost see a pair of white eggs in the hollow gnarled branches, so set forth with a friend after school. I had climbed the tree before, so that proved no problem, but twenty feet up a small branch broke, and there I was impaled, a leg each side of a barbed wire fence. I remember looking down and seeing small rings of flesh protruding from cuts on each leg. My friend in part panic shouted something, and took off to

Bindweed on Dock.

29

tell 'G', who was at that time milking just across the meadow at the mill. Running home, which was on the other side of the village, I particularly remember my boots filling with blood, and it seemed only minutes before 'G' had arrived on his bicycle. He strode in, a look of anger on his face, and said, 'I told you that you were in for a hiding if you climbed trees, so here goes'. With that he gave me two thunderous blows, one on each ear, and said, 'Fetch me the peroxide, Ada'. This he poured in each wound; having done this he strode off to resume his milking. I carry the scars to this day, for hardly ever were stitches then used, and I had to hobble over Middle Field (now Dunstall) to Dr. Longden, who was then the village doctor. In retrospect I think 'G' was a little heavy handed.

Most boys set brick traps in the garden, and would run home from school to see if they had caught any sparrows. The traps were made with four bricks and three small pieces of

Manor Cottage, 1926.

wood. The bird would be lured in with a little corn or crumbs of bread. Many were trapped this way and mostly alive, which was lucky, for if we caught an unsuspecting robin it could be loosed.

In the quiet spring evenings I could lie in bed at Manor Cottage and with the window open at dusk the nightingale would sing, slowly and shyly at first, then breaking into its beautiful full song which rolled up to the house in great waves like the washing of silent tides. Each year it came, for many years in the path at the bottom of the meadow called Marriot's Alley in between houses numbers 46–48. This footpath struck across Manor Road skewing down to Bedford Road, coming out a hundred yards south of Higham Road. It was hedged each side by very tall whitethorns; those double hedgerows were very favoured by nightingales, they preferred them to woodlands. We used to reckon on them singing in three places, one was Marriot's Alley, another Nobby Gate and the other was somewhere near the Bin. This is a group of trees south-east of Washbrook and south of the new cemetery and Lovers Walks.

Old Cottage, Manor Road.

Any night at mating time one could hear this wonderful sound, even the gruff horsekeeper would say quietly, 'I heard the nightingale sing last night'. I often saw them on my way home from school, very unobtrusive and common looking, mostly dull grey in colour and slightly light on the under parts.

> The wind blows here in the highest tree
> Where greenest lynchets lie,
> Over violets and wood anemone
> Here the woodcocks fly.
>
> On twisted roots tread carefully
> Or on their roots may fall,
> That twist and lap unsociably
> 'Neath the beeches tall.
>
> A dog at heel for company,
> The setting sun's afire
> Through trees that play a symphony,
> What more can man desire.

The nests were near to the ground and difficult to find, but these eggs were never taken even if found. The robin too had our protection. Children always said that to take a robin's egg would mean breaking a limb. I rather suspect that this rumour was started by our elders to protect such charming confiding birds. Each garden had a pair, and their songs, even on a sharp autumn evening, would be the only bird song to be heard. Perhaps someone still remembers the old rhyme.

> The Robin or the Redbreast
> The Robin and the Wren
> If ye take out o' their nests
> Ye'll never thrive again.
>
> The Robin or the Redbreast
> The Martin and the Swallow
> If ye touch one o' their eggs
> Bad luck will surely follow.

The most beautiful nest of all is quite rare but most rewarding to find. It is that of the long-tailed tit, a small round jewel of a nest hanging in the centre of briars, made of lichen and mosses and small feathers, also spiders' webs which are necessary, for as the young, which would be up to ten, grow, so the nest expands with their growing bodies, the lichens joined with cobwebs giving their home elasticity. Up in the open corn fields we searched for peewits' eggs, beautifully marked, dark putty blotched heavily with black. It took a trained eye and cunning to find these, but it was well worth the effort. In later years spending hours cultivating the land I found them my sole companions. They would walk sideways with inquisitive indifference a few yards from the tractor, seeming to display a mild interest. By the time one had worked the land through several operations, tineing, harrowing and drilling, their eggs would have to be moved several times. Making a little depression for the eggs, I would perhaps move half a dozen nests this way, and so save at least a dozen a year. Doing twenty-five years' farming, this made a considerable few, I like to think. Their mating flight involved soaring together, almost touching their breasts like two fluttering butterflies, or swooping evolutions, suddenly alighting and, with their little white waistcoats hollowing the soft soil, their crests would quiver and bend in the sharp east winds which, without fail, came to dry out the muddy clay morass in early spring.

> I have three names
> Said the Plover.
> Plover, Land Gull
> And another.

The saving of these precious eggs had a disadvantage, for often if there was any ploughing at hatching time, the parent birds would bring along their offspring in search of food in the newly sliced furrow. The adult birds would jump out and leave the small chicks behind. As the giant tractor wheels bore down on them and to a thunderous roar from the engine, the chicks would run and fall over the clods of earth, their long legs kicking in the air, showing little white powderpuff undersides, or they would sit tight hoping the grey mottled coats of fluff would not be seen. One didn't feel so kindly disposed towards them then. The tractor didn't take much to stop with three mould boards in the ground, but to jump off and catch these young birds, move them twenty yards, only to find them returned after a bout* or two would be rather disconcerting.

Another old superstition was not to look at a single crow, for we always said a little rhyme to one another when we saw crows in small numbers.

> One crow sorrow,
> Two crows joy,
> Three crows a letter,
> Four crows a boy.

It was also considered unlucky to see a magpie on its own. These birds, perhaps one of the prettiest in flight, are also one of the craftiest. They have a distinct liking for other birds' eggs, but try to cover their own up with an impenetrable hood of thorns.

> One is sorrow,
> Two is joy,
> Three is a wedding,
> Four is a birth,
> Five is silver,
> Six is gold,
> Seven is a secret
> > Never to be told.

In the shady and damp ditches grew the flower Herb Robert. This was known to us as headache flower, for to look at this hairy flower was supposed to give one a headache. To pick dandelion flowers was supposed to make children wet the bed, but they were picked in the spring by the basketful for it was time for making wine. An assortment of various flowers, later fruits were needed – cowslips, elderflowers and dandelion being the favourites. In the autumn we would collect hip fruits of the dog rose, elderberries, crab apples for jam, wild sloe, and

Herb Robert.

bullace*. Most houses had some sort of home-made wine for the grown-ups.

During this time 'G' would be busy drilling the corn and harrowing the meadows, walking miles behind the horses. He would ease his boots off in the evening with a big sigh. Invariably round his toe or round a corn, he would have a little sheep's-wool collected from some briars, a few leaves from the silver leaf which were very soft and supposed to be healing.

The warm spring rain would transform the countryside overnight, leaves would be growing, and a profusion of flowers. The orchards would become pink and white with petals, and the tall pear trees, with high pinnacles of snowy blossom, would stand elegant; sap would rise and the blood too. They used to say, when elder leaves were as big as a mouse's ears, a young man's fancy turned to other things.

'Is it true'
　　said the Dove,
'I've the sweetest
　　voice of love?'

Dog Rose.

Haytime

Warm nights and rain would make the grasses grow, until haytime would be here. The first week in April usually saw the first swallows followed by the house martins, swifts and sand martins. The coming of the turtle dove was heralded by its soft dulcet call. The meadows had to be cut with horses and mowing machines, but often 'G' would take over orchards for the grass as well as the apples. However, there was little room for horses in the orchards so these had to be mown with scythes, and in the hot sun, out of any breeze, this was a very hot and tiresome job. I remember 'G' having sun stroke after helping with the hay in Manor Orchard. Any load of hay came in handy with cows and calves to feed over the winter months.

Two horses cut the meadows pulling the grass machine, the tread on the cast iron wheels providing the power transmitted through a connecting rod to the cutting knife and helped by a man's weight on the seat. It was a wonderful sound to hear the scissor action of the knife, and, when the horses turned and reversed slightly at the corners into the swath again, the spring pawls would click, click, hypnotically on, a noise that unaccountably blended into the country sounds. Swallows dive and criss-cross after disturbed insects, multi-coloured butterflies and moths flit in alarm, thick blue and pink pollen shakes from the grasses in tiny showers of pastel shades, as the knife severs the flower stalks which stand fractionally before falling in neat rows, pushed into lines or swaths by the swath board.

Buttercups, dog-daisies, self-heal, fragrant orchids, knapweed, ladies smock, and many others all fall before the knife's shearing blade, as the patient horses walk round their ever decreasing square. A rabbit would run for cover showing its white scuff – signal for danger, and the first swaths would already be wilting under the heat of the day.

Very few small farmers had swath turners, or side delivery rakes, in those days, so that hay had to be made by hand, weather permitting, often turned by hand and cocked. These hay cocks were best left a few days to settle. To make them they had to be built up in layers, each above the other in neat conical mounds so that they picked up well – like buns, the old folk used to say.

Great pitch forks used to be handled with dexterity, over six feet in length with huge prongs; these would be jabbed into the top of the hay cock, and if they were small the first would be carried onto the next, so picking up two at a time, with two over-zealous and strong pitchers bundling them up. It was easy to get snowed under and it took all one's time to clamber out of the middle of the load, let alone keep it full and tread the load down well. 'G' would shout, 'Keep your middle full boy! Where do you warnt it, ubber* or ipper*?' He had a very irritating and disconcerting habit of going on before the horse to the next hay cock, so that before you had regained your balance (for it could be like riding on a wobbly jelly) he would hurl up a huge forkful of hay, almost submerging you. This he also did with sheaves at harvest, much to everyone's annoyance – his way of getting on with it, I suppose.

If there was a brook handy he would empty a couple of bottles of Burgess minerals in to a milk can with a little water in it, and place this in the brook to keep cool, for beaver time. I would be sent for this and would have a sly swig behind the hedge, and replace it with a little water. Once I delivered the goods it was painful watching each one slaking his thirst in turn, and me with parched throat being last in peck order; especially as being the youngest and smallest I probably worked harder than anyone, and it used to be agony to wait, until there was very little left.

> I fly very fast,
>> Said the partridge,
> And have wasted
>> Many a cartridge.

Clover hay was grown mostly for winter feed for the horses, and had different characteristics If standing, it cut well with nice juicy hollow stalks; many partridge would be cut from their nests and on occasions pheasants, too. The odd hare would find the cover convenient and would

HAZEL SPLIT
HURDLE MAKING

HAY
KNIFE

run in and out of the standing clover until, convinced its cover was disappearing and having had enough, it would lope off to some nearby corn. To cock clover hay we usually had three working together taking three rows; the centre being slightly in front would fork along the row making about a third of a cock, being called the cockrow, while the other two behind put theirs also on the same cock and would carry on round and round the field in this fashion.

The pace was set by the one in front and centre and as the pace hardly every slackened, the boy was usually given, or rather made to take, the centre row. One was consoled slightly by the fact that clover hung together much better than shiny grass.

Cows and Horses

Coloured cows came pattering
With the milk pails clattering,
Their cloven tread
Heard from my bed,
With all the sparrows chattering.

With land south, east and west of the village, and with milking needed twice a day as well as a milk round, there were busy times between hay and harvest. Leisure became scarce, tempers often short, growing up became and was looked on with pessimism rather than optimism. If one looked questioningly after being given an order, 'G' always had the same retort – 'I had to do it before I was your age'. One quickly learned not to argue with one's elders.

One of our prime tasks was milking the cows. There was always one cow that was an easy milker, nice and quiet. We had to learn on these, and what a wrist aching job it was, until one's wrists became accustomed to it. I used to feel proud when the first froth began to rise in the bucket, one felt really efficient, and when a friend looked over the door and was met with a well-aimed jet of milk in the face, it usually caused a great deal of laughter. Milk was taken round in five gallon cans with handles of brass and a name plate of brass soldered on the side. Two measures would hang outside – one pint and half a pint. A few years of this, especially with one can, would make the bicycle ride with a definite bias. The first houses on the list would receive the milk warm, for there were no coolers in those days. Sunday mornings it was not unusual to knock on a door, and someone would call out 'Come in and help yourself', and though the whole family was sat having breakfast, one would walk by them into the pantry on the far side of the room, find a jug, put in the required amount, have a chat, and carry on to the next house. Everyone wanted extra on Sundays, and no-one understood why the cows didn't give extra on that day to accommodate them.

Some of the cows' names come to mind – Jean, Daisy, Eileen, Chloe, Lily, Mary, Guy (born November 5th), Burrows, Bluebell, Janie, Zoe, Faith, Hope and Charity. My wife's sister, being named Eileen, was always embarrassed when we said 'that is Eileen', perhaps because of the size of her tits. They used to call them 'windy titted' in those days, the cows of course. There were times when they were called other unmentionable names, of course. 'G' bought a little Ayrshire cow, which always had twins. She was called Littl'un – a star turn and favourite. When calved, no fence could keep her away from her offspring; she always got through barbed wire to the hayricks without cutting herself. It was a year or two before I spotted how this was done. She would first push through her head and neck, then carefully place her foot on the middle strand, then passing through would replace her front foot with the rear one, thus passing safely through unscathed. It was mystifying to see her feeding placidly at the hay rick, the barbed wire still intact. When she was in season we had to take her to the bull at Streatley, and as we were allowed to lead her, I or another young lad would jump on her back and off she would go, knowing the way with no trouble, a mile and a half each way with just a hemp halter on.

Another cow, Lily, which 'G' went to purchase from the village Lilley, posed a problem. After the sale 'G' tied her behind the cart, but she just stood her ground, breaking the rope, and after a few quick turns round the ten acres meadow, was captured and tied again. All to no avail. She just dug in her feet, and in the end a cattle truck was the only remedy. She could be milked for a few weeks with perfect composure and impunity, then she would strike, so suddenly you couldn't see her leg move, into the milk pail, which was hurled across the cowhouse with a dreadful clatter; the milker covered in milk would usually have to pick himself off the floor, pride wounded, and with a great timidity have another try. We all thought that given time she'd quieten down. Trust, care and kindness were showered on her, and much respect, but it was no good. After a few weeks she'd strike again. We renamed her Sudden after a well-known cowboy character of that time, and she was approached like a boy wooing his first sweetheart. This nervous state was of course transmitted through the cow's teats, and when one started to relax – which was seldom – one's mind would begin to wander – she would strike with lightning rapidity by unleashing her leg with a forward movement and strike back almost in one sweet movement. One had a real scramble to gain one's equilibrium, for, expecting a good hiding after so many repetitions of her misdemeanours, she would excrete fluid all over. 'G' would say all you need is a little patience, but after a few unsuccessful attempts, with his leggings almost torn from his legs, certainly turned back to front, he decided she was not playing the game. He didn't go much on it either, so the rota was mysteriously changed and he never again had the pleasure. She was sold at Bedford Market and we all rather hoped she would not reach her next lactation.

As well as help with the cows I was often needed to put the horses into harness, the collars always being difficult for a young lad, or to stick the tails through the cruppers*, tying the wantry* belly bands. One huge white Clydesdale horse, who couldn't back a load, used to frighten me. He would almost sit on his backside in the breeching, his huge hairy feet smacking in the mud. I always hid behind the hovel whilst this was going on. If a cow was queer it usually meant a drench, but if it was a horse it meant stomach trouble, so one had to walk it. 'Keep it moving' 'G' would say. More often than not it would be a Saturday, for it was Sunday when the cows broke out, and as one grew older it was very aggravating to spend your Saturday night off walking a horse round a meadow, awaiting a fart which would trigger off some sort of stomach movement, and with luck would release oneself for the evening. During the busy times 'G' would employ a horse keeper, for the horses had to be fed, their tails plaited with straw, and groomed till they shone, while they were having their first halt. One huge man who helped was reckoned to be able to eat three dinners at a time; his appetite matched his enormous figure, and as we had a tree of Allington Pippins just outside the stable (an apple that always eats hard), it gave me much delight to see him champ these down three or four at a time, and smacking his lips as he did so – not dissimilar to 'Desperate Dan'.

When one became old enough, before driving a horse with lines (reins), first one had to lead the horse at 'horse hoe' up and down the field all day. This could become tedious, with a hard-mouthed horse champing at the bit, slobbering green slime over your head, taking the blame as usual for every displaced bean and mangold. I would look hopefully at 'G', wondering about finishing time. If I dared to ask about the time, he would say 'this one and then'. At that age one always thought he meant this one and then we will go home, but after traversing the row again, one would look enquiringly and say, 'I thought we were going going home after that row', and he would reply, 'I meant this one and then, another'.

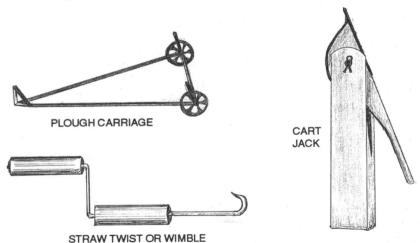

PLOUGH CARRIAGE

STRAW TWIST OR WIMBLE

CART JACK

Eventually I could use a fork either-handed and 'G' said such a man would be worth a shilling a week more; this did not however make any difference to my wages!

Country Characters

The pipe was short, the bowl burnt black,
The seat was broken where the old man sat,
But the smoke smelt good, as it lazed in the air,
When the lips retracted, and he blew with care.

In a Bedfordshire village 'neath the shade of a tree
He perched like an owl in a place he could see,
The acres before him where once he was hired,
In the clay soil and meadows before he retired.

He was young once again with hoe and rake,
In corduroy trousers the horse would take,
And no better team, with no better hand
Yet, ploughed such a furrow so straight in the land.

With his pint of ale, his square of meat,
Champing bits and the iron shod feet,
Unhook the lines, loosen the girth,
To the plough put your feet, kick off the earth.

The evening flows with the setting sun,
Sing a song in the lane as back you would come,
Happy, yet tired, and eager to see
Your wife at your table, set ready for tea.

Then down the damp paths where kingfishers flew,
Setting your snares where the wild brambles grew,
To tickle the trout in musical streams,
Quietly, patient, alone with your dreams.

Now that life has gone, departed like colour,
Little left but your pint and tobacco,
Few savings left to live at your ease,
No money from poaching to spend as you please.

> Live on your pittance, some cheese and a pint,
> Your age-worn dreams, a fast fading light,
> Lived with emotions, may welcome the day
> To travel those clouds, to a land far away.

Stories used somehow to circulate, who started them no one knew. Many tales were about one character who was supposed to have done many peculiar things, to say the least, some of which I remember. The time when he put the white cat outside to see if it was snowing. He was also supposed to have purchased a flashlight, or torch as it is called today, to light his pipe with. Once he said he's been out shooting, and the only rabbit he had shot was a hare that flew away. He told the doctor he had stomach trouble, not being able to pass anything. After having medicine for several days, he returned to the doctor who asked him 'Have you passed anything?' 'Yes,' he replied, 'a load of hay outside.'

Another small farmer used to broadcast his corn out of a bowler hat, and another harrowed corn with harrows tied behind his motor cycle and sidecar. One man who used to live in a caravan in about three acres of machinery which he was always going to do up, had a few acres, and with his own thrashing drum and tractor, used to thresh his corn on his own, throwing a few sheaves in the drum, then hopping down to shake up his corn sacks, rake out his cavings and clear away his straw. This was really labour saving, though somewhat tedious in practice. One farmer had a litter of kittens in his bowler hat, he took them out, he said, so that they wouldn't get 'round shouldered'! In the days of no TV in a small village, these tales were considered hilarious and soon spread.

After the 1918 war many men had an acre of ground to start on. One man a little more inventive than the others had a special hoe made, for in those days most corn was hand hoed; this particular man had a double one made to do his work twice as fast – I'm told he was the first to go bankrupt.

The fields being yellow with charlock two men were sent charlock heading. After several days a good divisional line could be seen from one end of the field to the other. The two men, filled with devilment, thought they could play a prank on the boss who they knew would be round after they had gone home. They hacked two pieces out of the hedgerow about six feet tall and stuck them up each end of the field at the place where they left off. The next day the boss was soon round. 'What are these two pieces of wood for?' he asked. 'So's we know where we left off' they replied in all immaculate innocence. They were both fired.

Two lads seeing which one could throw the farthest, the younger smaller one constantly threw further than the older, who, in desperation said 'Ha, I can't throw very well in these shoes'.

Farmer, seeing his horse lying dead in the stable, turned to his hired help and said 'It's the first time that its played that trick on me'.

Two farmers discussing a sick donkey. 'It's right off its food,' said the first man. 'It won't hurt,' said the second, 'it's said you get used to everything in time. Try leaving it without food altogether.' They met about a month later. 'How's the donkey?' said the second farmer. 'Had a bit of bad luck,' said the first. 'I left it without food as you suggested, and it was just getting used to it, when it went and died.'

A Mr Gardner, a farmer new to the village, was known, among other things, for his strength. A carter was going to his farm with horse and cart for a load of wheat, which was measured in two-and-a-quarter-hundredweight sacks. He asked the carter what he would rather do – stack the corn in the cart or lift them up from ground level with no other aid but his own strength. The carter chose the first of course. Later he asked the man if he would like a drink. 'Yes please,' he said, thinking a jug of beer would be forthcoming. 'Alright,' said Mr Gardner, taking him to the pump. 'I'll pump, you cup your hands.'

> At the closing of the day
> When first rabbits are at play,
> Lovers with their hands held tight
> Walk slowly on a starlit night,

Fingers feel a lover's pledge,
Steal kisses there behind the hedge,
Ne'er feel the chill in cold moon's light,
In ecstacy cling till deep into the night.
Frantic if their passion's not complete,
Forgetting all the other times they'll meet.

A traveller used to call at the cottage about twice a year selling his home made corn ointment. Mother had implicit faith in its healing qualities, we always teased her about this and used to ask 'Has old Ointment been to see you lately?' What amused us most was that he used to produce from his waistcoat pocket a large corn, which had fallen from his own toe, and this was larger than a field bean and irregular in shape. We doubted his integrity but did suggest that he should have it mounted in a ring.

'G' decided one day to launch out. Not many had wireless in those days and as we had a wireless mechanic in the village, he decided to give him a try. After much talk it was finally decided, he would make up a wireless for 'G' using an old treadle sewing machine cover to encase it, putting a little speaker in the front. We had to use earphones, however, and as there was not

The Old Lockup.

one each, we sat on edge to hear the first sound of music through such a modern marvel. Later we had the set modernised and could hear through the speaker; this must have been in the middle twenties.

In those times a visit from the owners of the Manor House opposite was considered a highlight and honour. Once or twice we were asked over, and at Christmas they would pay us a visit. 'G' would be given a cigar and us children half-a-crown each, which was more than we got all the year at any one time. Our very best behaviour was called for each time, for 'G' was inclined to be a bit of a snob himself.

Mr and Mrs Smurthwaite who lived at the Manor had a dear old companion help who spent most of her evenings off in our presence and would act as a sort of babysitter if Mother and Father went to the Celebrity Concerts in Luton. She would read to us, and it would amuse us greatly when she came across longish words for she would gabble over them, and of course, pretending we hadn't heard properly, we would ask her to repeat them. We would escort her to Chapel on Sunday evenings when she would always have her torch on all the way down the lane, though it was always across her arm shining in the hedge almost behind her, quite useless, but she would never alter the beam direction. She had a habit of always finishing her sentences with 'an do it', being of Yorkshire stock.

Hens In The Orchard

I once had a hoop,
A hen in a coop,
A conker on a string,
A catapult I made myself,
But couldn't hit a thing.

We always had a few hens of various sorts. Being interested now and again 'G' would have a sitting of Houdan eggs, lovely speckled birds with a large tassel on their heads, and an extra claw. These characteristics took years to die out, chickens of all sorts having tassels, though slightly smaller.

Two cockerels I remember well. One was kept down the Mill, and, hearing anyone walking down the lane on the ashed road, would wait at the end and fly straight into their backs. This was disconcerting for anyone who had two buckets of water on yokes to carry home. 'G' was under considerable pressure to get rid of the bird concerned, but he was very reluctant to do this for, as he said, it kept the boys away far better than a bull running wild. The other one he kept up the Orchard and this was a little 'Ancona' which took a dislike to 'G's' leggings and would literally take a running jump at them. 'I've seen 'G' carry a stick and clout the cockerel's head so hard it would knock it out and it would lie on its back as if dead. 'That will teach you,' 'G' would say, but on returning it would jump up, shake its head as though still groggy, and would go for 'G' again, with renewed vigour. The one thing that 'G' could do, that I never could, was to wring a chicken's neck in a split second. Many locals would bring one round and say 'wring its neck George, will you?'

One particular incident I remember; a partridge befriended our hens and would be with them all day chisicking when anyone came near and only running a few yards away when they were fed. At night it would sit in the 'pop hole' until morning. It was with them for months, but disappeared one Saturday morning while we were at Bedford Market.

Where bowered blossoms of the May
Throw tinted petals on the way,
And tufted grasses swirled on high
Like the zig zag flight of the butterfly.
Where the wild winds sweet and strong
The skylark's lovely song.
A lone hare treads its uphill run
Disappearing in the setting sun.

✦ ✦ ✦ ✦ ✦

The wildest of flowers
Catch a light from his eye,
Leave their fragrance on
    boots
When he jostles them by.

The touch of the earth
When his fingers caress,
Is to him like a girl
When she feels her new dress.

The huge beef shoulders
That square the male,
The straight backed heifer
With thin hanging tail.

Or the cool soft nose
Of seeking calf.
The feel of eggs
Hidden in chaff.

The rustle of straw
Where his knees gently stir,
By the new born he kneels
To wipe dry the fur.

Woody Nightshade.

Hexton Road. Pound Pond was here.

'G' had a henhouse up in the Hexton fields, nearer to Hexton than Barton. He would put some poultry there in the autumn when the corn had been carted, and though there was a chain and an old gin trap hanging over the 'pophole', I had to run up there each evening just before dark to shut them up for the night or the fox would have raided. I tried to arrive just at dusk, but usually there would be one hen still out, prowling around the hen house for no apparent reason. If it saw you it would come running, if you tried to drive it down, the others would hear it and with a flapping of wings would all rush out being inquisitive. One had to hide behind the hedge or they would just stand with a blind curiosity and stare. This henhouse came in handy for pigeon shooting when not occupied with hens, for it stood near an ash tree, the only one for half a mile and much sought after by the marauding pigeons. With part of the roof removed one could sit in this strategic position on a nest box out of wind and rain and just wait for the pigeons. This sport, however, was short lived. The owner of the tree, for reasons known only to himself, had the tree cut down.

'G' would often return home after plucking chickens with a few of their predators still on him. 'They're just going over my skating rink', he would say, and I would jump up and click a flea with my nails.

> You declare your departure
> From my woollen seams,
> A rude interceptor
> Of agreeable dreams.
> So I furiously grope
> For the small parasites
> That reluctant I carry
> And succour by night.

Henhouses up in the Orchard were rather dilapidated and rarely cleaned out. Odd lumps of iron were thrown on the roofs to keep on the loose corrugated iron, wheel, axles, pieces of stone, the weight alone was sufficient to collapse the roofs in. The hollows made by the weight caught the leaves and rattled the roofs, so the hens spent most of their lives huddled up one end or another. Hens of various breeds would perch where they could, some on the nest boxes and some even in them, which all made comfortable nesting, but clean eggs impossible. This made some hens seek seclusion for their egg laying in remote places, so that egg collecting became more like finding hidden treasure. We always had volunteers to collect the eggs, and the favourite trick was to let them see you collect them from one or two nice quiet sitters and then dare them to do the same from under one known to be spiteful. I would on occasions show off a bit if 'G' wasn't in the offing, by showing a friend how to put a hen to sleep, tucking its head under a wing, and holding it tight with both hands, head under the wing, and by gently wafting it round in circles, three or four times, place it on the ground where it would remain, head under wing for several minutes, before recovering and running off.

The orchard (now Blakelands), about one quarter acre, had many old fruit trees, cart hovel, trolley hovel, a long hut, stables and chaff house, also sundry other buildings, along with the henhouses and the remains of a garden at the bottom end where roses, daffodils and snowdrops grew. The remains of three dwelling houses have been found there since. On some old deeds I have, it states one was let for the princely sum of 2/8d per year. We had a well, too. The water was drawn from this to water the horses, but it had a definite tang, for the sewer was pumped out weekly along a wooden duct into the open meadow about fifty yards from the well; all animals seem to relish its flavour. 'G' told me that when he first bought the Orchard someone had used the well to dump rubbish in, so he decided to clean it out. All the blue-black slurry was taken by bucket and dumped round the fruit trees. It was the source of some humour later when it turned out to be full of charlock seeds and every tree had a beautiful golden surround when the charlock bloomed. How long it had been down there was anyone's guess. He told me how he once dropped his pocket watch down there, and after emptying the well with buckets, he found the watch, the glass broken but still going.

We did find time once in a while to play, and more than often it was up in the Orchard. We would climb in the hovels looking for sparrow's nests, build houses with empty chaff bags over the stable, and jump down into the chaff. It made a soft landing, but filled everything worn with chaff. Swallows built regularly in the open sheds. We nailed pieces of wood under the beams for them to nest on in comparative safety.

> In sullen pools
>> The searching moorhens swim
> On rafter nest,
>> The rushes that they bring
> To brown, the colour
>> That their nest will be,
> Low in the reed
>> That prying eyes will never see.
> Ten brown blotched eggs
>> Lying in her care.
> I only know that they are there
> And only I can tell you where.

There was a pigeon house nailed up on the stable, which always seemed supplemented with strays. When 'G' wanted a couple we used to shoot them off the top of the stable with a four-ten shotgun. The metal ridging became peppered with holes, so bad that 'G' forbade this practice and we had to have a ladder and catch them in the dark, or before they were old enough to fly.

Slightly more exotically peacocks were kept at the nearby Manor, but spent most of their time in our garden or roosting on the top of the cottage, which was always the signal for their raucous and unearthly screeching. We had a little bantam cock at the time called Stribling (after a boxer of that time) and he hated the sight of these peacocks and would lunge himself at their throats and just hang on while they pulled him round hanging apparently lifeless. Their beautiful tail feathers were never allowed in the house as they were considered unlucky.

They also kept two lovely trout in the pond, which swam leisurely to the side for food at the sound of clapping hands. These unfortunately met an untimely end. While the pond was being cleaned they were put in the sunken garden but didn't survive. The water was stocked several times with other fish, but these were taken by marauding herons. I could sometimes hear their wings as I lay in bed at dusk, circling round to see if it was safe to land. Unfortunately, as the old folks used to say, 'their eyes were bigger than their guts' and they would kill more than they wanted. I also remember eels being caught in the pond, two to two-and-a-half feet long, and left hanging wriggling in our barn.

Our water was carted in buckets on yokes from the brook at the rear of the Manor. 'Pump Yard' was a daily lark, and as children we would spend time, when we could, standing on stones trying to catch Milla thumbs, a small thumb-like fish, which would dart from stone to stone with great rapidity and if unlucky finish up in our water butt where its life expectancy was very short.

Streams and Straw Plait

Hear the purest water falling
Where the speckled songthrush sings,
In the valley there in Barton
Of the cold and laughing springs.

'Neath the elms and elder twisting
Through the chalk hills fill the stream,
O'er smooth stones, by the kingcups,
Wash the shaded celandine.

Little dams made by the children,
Water wheels of sticks were made.
Hear the pigeon's soft note calling,
Lords and ladies in the shade.

Many lips cooled with her kisses
Many hands have cupped her water,
Young and old sat down beside her
Where the flowers look out to Summer.

At one time our natural beauty spot was desecrated, having
iron pipes shoved into the springs themselves. This was about
the greatest single act of vandalism ever perpetrated by any one
person in the village, and all just to give one household fresh
water. After a year or two the piping was broken, the water
escaping as it does to this day.

'G' would tell me of the times when, at the outlet of the
springs, watercress was grown. The shape of these beds can still
be seen faintly outlined.

Water Cress Beds, Barton Springs.

Barton Springs

The cress was fed by the hills, they say,
Water that sang in a yesterday,
Drained through the chalk hills crystal clear,
Down through beeches standing near,
Moss greened shafts through winter's way
Or emerald leaved, on a bright Spring day.

Boisterous tinkling, melodious streams,
If only I knew what your laughter means,
If you'd just tell your secrets to me
Before running down to the estuary,
Absconding your way to the grey blue sea,
Your braided lights in a ripple flow
To the far horizon downward go.

On our walks there could be a special treat. 'G' would put his hand in his pocket and pass over a sweet for all. He would tell of how his Mother would, when walking with other women of the village, hold straws in her mouth to keep them pliable, and would separate them with little straw splits, chines or cheens, and plait the straw together as they walked. This they would roll flat with wooden roller plaitmills which usually hung outside their back doors. This was sold to the hat manufacturers in Luton for a few pence. Many women walked the seven miles into Luton to sell their plait on market day, Monday, and once there would hold it out between their hands for the buyers to peruse. Different prices given according to neatness or fineness. Some children were sent to a straw school, in someone's barn, at the age of three, to learn the trade. In later years young girls walked through the yellow meadows of buttercups in the warm evenings, chatting and plaiting, often with some assignation; a lad would meet them and many a courtship started this way.

In the twenties and thirties many ladies supplemented their husband's low wages by having the plait delivered to their door and would sit for hours machining it into straw hats. It must be remembered that at that time Luton was the principal hat manufacturer in England; many of the inner streets

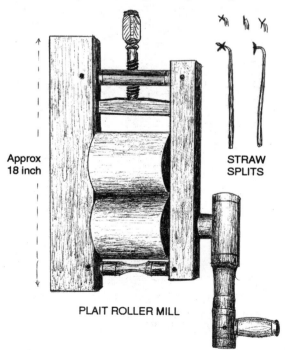

Approx 18 inch

STRAW SPLITS

PLAIT ROLLER MILL

were filled with their factories. They, like the farmers, one heard, never made any profit! Up to a few years ago many homes in the village had hat machines, but little is done today.

'G' would also talk of the Grandfather, who was one of the few working men who could write his own name, and how he would get his scythe down and get a razor edge on it, ready for going, as he put it, 'down the hay country', which meant leaving home for several months to scythe in the hayfields. He would talk of bird scaring for the odd halfpenny or farthing, running round the cornfields shouting if he hadn't a clatterer, and of a neighbouring farmer who played a piccolo to scare the birds. Perhaps he did it for a lark?

We children would walk and run back on the west side of the water, jumping over the little waterfalls where the stream ran narrow, and looking for rarer flowers. Kingcups grew in one spot then, and still grow there forty-five years later. Just before we reached the rear of the new cemetery over the old

Hare Bell.

culvert, which was probably the only way of fording the stream to the south, we would pick primroses down by the stream or on 'primrose hill', a hill which is now covered in white thorn scrub and long ant hills. Bluebells remain, showing their resilience over many years of plundering by eager young hands.

Down by the banks
    By the water force
I once saw a man
    On a bright blue horse,
With reins of forgetmenots
    Laced with gold
He held them out
    For me to hold.
I've watched you bluebelling
    Said he,
Are there a few
    You could spare for me?
For I live far away
    Up in the skies
But saw bells of blue
    Reflect in your eyes.
That some of the blue will
    Remain there I've planned
And some of their fragrance
    Remain on your hands.

Summer draws near, and the lull before the storm. Days when with a clear sky and blowing wind, on a Monday morning everyone would be astir, a good drying day, the women folk having their coppers filled in readiness for the week's washing, and wearing hessian aprons, would light their fires under their coppers to boil the water, and with red soapy arms, rush to and fro in to the barns to start the washing. It was always done on a Monday, and with luck would be dry and folded for ironing next day. We could hear the flapping of sheets on the clothes line when passing and see a smile on the face of the washer women, all things being in accord.

While in the fields unfilled wheat ears peep like a child, in between their leaf curtains. Barley hales tiny green artist brushed bursting from swollen sheaths swaying in the wind, as a seaweed in changing ebb, or giant arms sweeping the green stalks in different ways, always escaping to swirl yet again to the far headlands. The top oat bells hand, some shine white and empty – is it sparrow, or the dreaded frit-fly? Field beans grow, their blue-green tops like rows of rabbit ears, with their bright-eyed flowers trod open by the bumble bees. In the soft fallows the hare presses in his form, the big brown eyes look up at the hovering kestrel, which in turn looks down with beady eyes at a field mouse scampering under the blue lucerne flowers.

The boys would block up the Washbrook stream for bathing and down west of the village the Meadhook stream would be blocked for swimming by the Boy Scouts who used to camp there during the summer. Before the hut just up the Sharpenhoe Road was given to them for a memorial, I believe, they used a small hut next to the Ramsey School, which was also used by a farmer, so that during summer it was often half filled with sacks of corn. I remember climbing over them to attend a Court of Honour. I had not been in the Scouts long before blotting my copybook. The local baker, having the name of Mr Hodge, one day while he was delivering his bread, I said 'Hello, Mr Hodge,' and getting no reply, I repeated 'Mr Hodge' and still he ignored me, so I said 'Mr Hodge' several times quickly, which to him sounded like Mr Stodge. Called a baker Stodge – I did not realise the humour until later. However I was dismissed by the Court of Honour after carefully explaining.

'G' would spend a few hours in the front garden trying to tidy up a little before harvest. Unfortunately he was not tidy-minded. He would splash about, dig almost everything up, weeds and flowers, having little preference. Mother would come behind him saying, watch this, and, mind that, and so it would go on, only the rose trees surviving and those only just. An uneasy friendship existed while 'G' was in the garden. Poor Mother! Her slips of flowers were doomed from the start, he just hadn't the love his brother 'Sarge' had for flowers, alas, whose advice was often sought by garden lovers. He always had his eye open for a briar or a wild crab. He would note the spot then during winter would dig them up, take them home to bud or graft – if a crab it would be his favourite apple or a rare good one he had heard of. Poor old Sarge, he had the 'Early Rivers' plum trees in his garden, but they would never yield like the one 'G' had. The one 'G' had was always surrounded by nettles and had harrows and all sorts propped up against it, but every year it bore much succulent fruit.

After Sarge's next door tenant moved, he decided to enlarge his lawn; the new grass was just growing, when our two horses decided to get loose, one being a huge shire. They decided by some devilish quirk, that the only damage they could do was to visit his garden. The holes they left on the newly sown lawn had to be seen to be believed, one could have dropped buckets in them. As they decided to leave, they knocked the top off the well. 'G' said 'It's a good job they didn't fall in'. Sarge said 'It's a pity they didn't'.

A few plants, cabbages, etc. would be planted and of course the inevitable hole for the night soil, a job which often kept me busy during the evening. I remember growing a good patch of lettuce while still a boy, all the hearts started turning in together. I thought how lucky I must have been and evidently 'G' had the same thoughts for on returning from school one evening, I ran greatly dismayed to find half of them out and gone. His friends were even luckier – he had given them away.

White and red currant trees were shrouded in old lace curtains to keep off the blackbirds, but often I watched them run through the long grass and creep up under the bottom of the curtains. I decided this was the best approach for me, too.

Harvest

Everything seemed to be geared up for the harvest. The oats would start to 'turn', the wheat would first become milky and so herald the sparrows from near and far. The binder would be uncovered, oiled, greased, and the canvases put on loosely, the binder carriage placed underneath, and all at the ready with new balls of string, placed in the string box, threaded through to hold that masterpiece of invention by a Canadian, MacCormick in 1831, which revolutionised the cutting of corn – the knotter. Mr A Brightman, who was old when 'G' was a child, told me that when the first binders and reapers came to the village south of Higham Road, all the locals collected to watch this mysterious machine which alleviated the need for scythes. These first reapers did not tie the sheaves but threw the corn out in neat rows. 'They'll never work' they said, shaking their heads. When a farmer started his farm with beautiful Suffolk horses they shook their heads and said, 'They won't be any good on this soil, their legs are too thin'. It's been thus ever since, with tractors which were too heavy for Barton clay and panned the soil, and later combines which threw more out the back than in the hopper, and again with hay balers which spoiled hay too easily. There was an element of truth in most of these arguments; until these implements were used efficiently, with practice and alterations, there was much misuse, of course, and waste. It was some time before their prejudice was allayed.

Corn, especially wheat, could be cut a little on the green side so that it ripened up in the stook. 'G' would sharpen up his scythes to 'mow round' so the horses would not spoil too much, and the binder the first time round. What a job that was! An untidy scyther meant the 'taker out', the one that tidied up the corn and tied the sheaves with straw, so that none was left behind on the headlands. Of course the corn was thinner, consequently the thistles or soldiers* stood taller and healthier. 'Seize 'em, boy', 'G' would say, 'They won't prick' but to straighten scythed corn using legs and arms, both almost bare, under a hedge on a hot day is well remembered by all the children who have been driven to this torture.

Poppy.

If oats looked ripe the old folks used to say 'Now's time for a week's holiday,' meaning that they were never as ripe as they looked. How I wished I had long trousers on when I first started this job. I used to roll down my sleeves, if I had any, to protect my arms a little, but the knees took a terrible scuffing, and to wash one's arms and legs at night was sheer agony.

At a much later date when we first pulled the binder with a shortened pole behind the tractor, I rode round without mowing by hand first. 'G' nearly went berserk after seeing the flattened corn, shook his head and stamped off, but by going the opposite way round after moving the sheaves out of the way, and lowering the table right down, hardly any corn was missed, the fingers lifting the corn which in turn lifted the straw lying over it, so with one piece of corn lifting the other, less was wasted than would have been with a scythe. 'G' was not convinced though it saved a day's heavy toil, or more. Throwing in would start when the binder had been round four times, for we threw in usually three rows either side into the middle, and two which we didn't have to move. This was called a 'shock row' or as they say in the Northern hemisphere a 'stook row.' This saved much time when shocking up a field, for it saved wandering out to pick up sheaves and carry them back into the row. The sheaves were shocked up by as many boys and men as were available, care taken to jab down 'arse' ends so that they stood better. We tried to keep them in line and each shock neat so that the wind could get through. About eight or ten was the usual even number, and one tried to 'marry' the ears a little so they stood against the wind.

One always enjoyed a little sport if a few rabbits were in the corn. They usually came out the first few times round, or were frightened in towards the centre where they eventually had to make a break for it. I always admired a good shot, it gave me much pleasure to see a professional stand and watch a rabbit run to a good range and perhaps just before it disappeared into the hedge, casually lift up the gun and over would roll the rabbit cleanly shot. Well do I remember the first twelve bore 'G' allowed me to use, after being weaned on an airgun, then later a four-ten gun. The twelve bore was an old hammer gun purchased at some farm sale years ago. Both barrels had been blown out halfway up, and the local blacksmith had wrapped an iron band 3/16" thick round the holes. The rest of the barrels were deeply pitted and were never cleaned, paper thin at the ends; the bands made the gun heavy and out of balance, and after more use one could see daylight through inside the barrels, where they were blowing again by the bands. For all this the gun was straight and a good killer, and I used it regularly, quite oblivious of the tremendous danger I was placing myself in. It was much later after the purchase of a better one that I became aware of my foolhardiness, for it must have been a potential killer in more ways than one.

> Revolving sails that stroke
> The golden ears
> Towards the slicing cutter knife
> That shears
> On turning canvas up and over,
> Packs for waiting fingers

Where flying butter boards
    Push the straw that lingers,
The knotter ties to safeguard
    Any waste,
While sheaves rejected
    In abandoned haste,
Rowed regimented in
    Waiting lines,
To await collection with the work worn tines.

If a good crop had been cut and shocked the field always looked full and they would say 'That field's shocked up well,' and it certainly would make the horses work overtime and the connecting rod clank, the butter boards knock while the rows of corn were stroked onto the bottom canvas by the sails, up and over the binder pressing down the tripper, the fingers turning and whacking out the sheaves with hardly a pause, sheaf after sheaf. The dog roses would still be hanging in the hedgerows, pink like choirboys' mouths singing a song; the disturbed hare would run straight through half a mile of runs, safely three of four fields away; a corncrake would creep stealthily away into the next standing crop; a dog runs through standing shocks head high in delight, rubbing its backside, and the first shock would fall. Someone would shout 'They're falling arse over head before we leave the field,' so all hands would work until the last piece of corn was knocked down and as much set up again, before knocking off time. When the corn was cut at the foot of the hills (the field called the Coombs) there would be so many rabbits, the keepers would erect wire netting round the lynchets to hold them back. Anything up to a hundred at a time could be caught, but he was a lucky boy who could chase and catch one with his stick, or even have one given him and proudly carry it home. Sometimes a little extra reward could come out way, the odd pheasant somehow fell to the gun. Great care had to be exercised however, for these game birds were not only out of season but treasured by the gamekeepers for later shoots, and as 'G' rented twenty acres from the Estate there was usually a keeper lurking about or having a panoramic view from the neighbouring hills. I well remember shooting a rabbit up a wide row of corn; when I picked it up I saw that a pheasant had been shot at the same time not many yards from a keeper. I picked up the rabbit and after the binder cut over the pheasant, kicked a sheaf sideways to mark the spot. This was the usual practice; they were picked up much later and popped in a sack.

It's always been a sore spot with me, that pheasant and partridge were bred and fed on one's own corn, and yet if one returned later, even in one's own back garden, an expensive game licence had to be taken out before one could shoot it. There are plenty of ways to prosecute any offender taking game unlawfully without this antiquated law that smells of pheasants for the Masters only. Not many countrymen with any land at all could truthfully say that they hadn't broken the law at some time or another, and I think it high time for rectification.

> Blue pigeons perch clawed
>> Throughout the night,
> All other birds await the morning light,
> With silence glide
>> To far-off fields to feed,
> Each to its own particular
>> Kind of need.

They call the Scarlet Pimpernel the poor man's weather guide, for if open they reckon it will be fine for the day. My Aunt Polly had some always growing by her back door and she wouldn't allow anyone to pull it up, having implicit faith in this tiny flower. It was always a good sign to see the flowers open during harvest, though I think they opened every fine day anyway. On some of the larger fields a third horse was used to cut the corn; chained to the front of the binder pole it would be called the 'forest horse'. When a forest was needed some unfortunate lad (usually me) had to ride it all day for it was difficult to guide the horse being so far in front and to manoeuvre it round corners. The forest seat on the front horse could be pure agony after the first hour or so. I remember the horse I had to ride, the angle of its protruding backbone has left an indelible print in my mind, among other things. A sack was thrown on its back and this had to suffice, hours of discomfort, its sharp bones and the sweat from the horse's ribs, rubbing and chafing my bare legs which would become wet with sweat and covered with loose horse hairs. Anything that disrupted the binder, whether horse or machine, was invariably blamed on the forest boy. One either turned too short or too long, or let the horse wander. I was always kept sustained whilst helping a neighbour by his repeated assurance that it was well worth sixpence by the end of the week. I can see that imagined sixpence now, for this was as near as I ever got to receiving it. One must realise that the smallholders and farmers hardly ever had these machines new, consequently they were almost at the end of their tether before purchase, and knotter and canvas trouble was the main bugbear, providing one had a pair of good horses.

> Ogee boy, Ogee boy,
> > Lead well your load
> Sunripe corn; grass
> > That was mowed,
> Stockings fall down
> > As you run down the road
> With great striding horse
> > Making light of its load.

I think next to riding a half-starved forest horse all day, the task of bean gleaning was next on that hate list, in fact it became a joke – if one had misbehaved someone would say, 'Watch it or you'll be sent bean gleaning.' When the binder had cut the field beans a few would be left behind, perhaps cleavers hung them on the sails or some would be rain beaten flat so that the knives only took off the tops, leaving stalks with the beans on behind. These had to be 'gleaned', a monotonous job where one had to take about four rows at a time, walk up and down all over the field bending up and down, up and down lashing the brittle stalks under the arm and depositing them in little sheaves, to be tied up at a later date, unless strings were tied around one's middle for this purpose. There never looked much to show for it; after days of this endless occupation only a few heaps of beans which when thrashed couldn't have made up more than half a bushel. If any were left 'G' would say, 'You haven't above half done them', or threaten that we would have to go over them yet again. Needless to say I was never convinced of the practicalities of bean gleaning but think it was done in the old tradition of 'Waste not, want not'. Many women gleaned the wheat in those days, in neat little tiny bundles, for their chickens, and if much corn was left the field would be horse dragged and so that no one hand gleaned it, one shock was left standing. This was an unwritten law and usually observed, meaning no gleaning, field not dragged. In olden days the wheat was collected by the women and family and taken to the miller for flour and they would often invite friends in to show, with pride, their flour, though it wasn't always looked on kindly by the farmers. There was an old law which stated gleanings should be left to the poor and strangers, so they couldn't do much about it. However, on some farms it was prohibited for

Mill Lane.

the workers to keep pigs in case a little other than gleaning was taken home. Wheels were taken off the carts yearly, for greasing; owing to their sideways slack they knocked a little. 'G' used to say, 'a lovely sound to hear a good cart knocking.'

Have I earned a penny, Dad,
     Taking out all day?
Yes, you have earned a penny, lad,
     Taking out all day.
With thistled hands
Tie straw held bands
     Yes, you have earned a penny, lad.

Have I earned a penny, Dad,
     Being an Ogee Boy?
Yes, you have earned a penny, lad,
     Being an Ogee Boy.
Held chap rein firm
How quick you learn
And walking all the day,
     Yes, you have earned a penny, lad.

Have I earned a penny, Dad
     Riding middle hoss?
Yes, you have earned a penny, lad.
     Riding middle hoss.
With sore backside
An eight hours' ride
And grumble from the boss,
     Yes, you have earned a penny, lad.

Have I earned a penny, Dad,
     Gleaning beans all day?
Yes, you have earned a penny lad,
     Gleaning beans all day.
Bean pods rattle in the sun
Told your work has been half done,
You've broken you heart and bit your tongue,
     Yes, you have earned a penny, lad.

Will I get a penny, Dad,
    At the end of summer?
Yes, you will get a penny, lad,
    At the end of summer.
With draggings won
The thatch well hung,
And days are getting shorter.
Come and see me then lad,
    At the end of summer.

We had a dog for a many years called Floss, a black bob-tailed bitch. She would walk round the village to call at friends and relations twice a week regularly for titbits. She slept anywhere that took her fancy up in the orchard, and was never shut in except when on heat. She was a good ratter and rabbiter with a true nose and of course a great favourite with us children. We knew if she was in whelp as she disappeared for a whole week; going down to the meadow one day she barked, and we found her with eight pups in the roots of an old elm tree. Any pups wanting their tails off, they used to say, would be done by biting. Apparently there was always the odd character in the village who would do this for a pint. Poor Floss met an untimely death. Whilst cutting wheat up at Hexton Field, she did the unforgivable by jumping in the corn after a rabbit in front of the binder. Before it could be halted, three of her legs were cut off. All we could do was to put her at rest with two barrels from the twelve bore, leaving us all heartbroken. I well remember once cutting corn at the Hexton field, packing up through rain and I had put my twelve bore gun under the table of the binder and inadvertently left it there. Floss was not to be found but going up to the field next day there she was, lying as close to the gun as she could; she had been there all night in the rain.

The next big job was corn cart. Straw would be shaken for a rick bottom; after the straw was shaken up the size would be assessed and sticks stuck in the corners. To start the rick a shock would be built in the centre and sheaves placed round the centre shock until the outside was reached. Thus the centre was kept high and allowance made for the rick to spread as it reached the eaves. Care was taken to always keep the centre full to throw out any water that could get in; each sheaf was lapped half its length by another so that the centre rose by a series of steps sloping down all round to the outside. If the weather held good, dinner would be had sitting in the nearest shade, and work would carry on until late that day.

> Drove the horse
>   And pitched the load
> So none would fall off in the road.
> Take horses home, hurrying
> For the light is worsening.
> The older men would dare to say
>   I've had enough
>   For this one day.

By the time one had walked home it would often be quite dark. The stars would shine like jewels in a stark velvet cloak when the day joins night in quiet communion. The lighted windows of home would indeed be a welcome. I would be washed in carbolic soap and be ready for bed by the time 'G' had racked up or turned out the horses for the night. Boys were enlisted to be ogee* boys; this was to drive the horse up the field, and lead by the chap rein* from shock to shock; as the ricks became high a hole would be left in the side of the rick where a man would stand, catch the sheaves and hurl them up on to the top. This was called a pitch hole. Sometimes a harrow would be embedded in the roof by its tines and someone would stand with heels in the bars to do the same job. When the roof became narrower sometimes above the top of the tallest ladder, some youth would say 'how do I get down?' and some wit would reply 'just close your eyes, boy, and walk about a bit.' The usual ricks in this area were oblong or round. Much later, with newer and heavier bearing wheat, which was larger at the ear ends than the bottom, I found building the corners difficult as the ears had to be pulled in together, so I built a Boston jug. I had heard my father talk of them, roughly oval in shape, and they made building much easier.

> Summer days refreshed by showers,
> Bumbles pushing heads in flowers,
> Pansies lift their heads to say
> This truly is a summer's day.
>> None should tend
>> but sit in shade,
> Hear the robins serenade.

I think oats were the most troublesome as they were so slippy one could shoot off a rick edge, like riding a magic carpet. If carted too soon they would overheat in the rick. Well did I remember 'G' building one where the open shed at Ramsay School is now, this being the old rick yard; we had to rebuild through overheating. It was a hot day and standing on the rick we were demolishing was like standing on an oven all day, the hottest I've ever been in this country at any rate. If there was a slight pause in the rhythm of unloading there was always someone who would say 'Can't you find the layers, boy?' 'Git your arse behind you' or 'Don't lift yourself.' One felt quite a man sitting in the empty carts, or sitting on the raves* with reins through the copses driving the horse through the village to the fields, and often collecting half a load of children. 'G' never to my recollection built a nice-looking rick, and often a few feet from the ground the rick would assume an early form of pregnancy, so one dare hardly mention the fact, but if someone said better get a lawyer* or Cranfield* man, or prop, he would glare. This is what it usually came to; once a few sheaves through careless treading came out of their binders, nothing would push them back again, however much whacking they received with a fork, and as the rick rose so they would slip dangerously further and further, much to everyone's suppressed mirth, too much rise-taking, and 'G' could be most annoyed, making work very unpleasant. In fact a thing like this could bring on a queer unexplained turn, everyone would work away and no words spoken, when 'G' had one of his turns. This extraordinary behaviour made things very unpleasant especially if any extra help was there and became unwittingly involved. On the half built ricks a huge rick cloth would be put during the night, with logs and ladders hanging on the ropes, the older men accused the younger boys of not pulling on the rope, but as it happened on one occasion the rope broke and the boy was the only one to fall over. Loading the carts was usually a boy's job, but with bad pitchers it would become a nightmare, and with short trousers the knees would collect thistles, so too the hands. The idea, of course, was to throw up the sheaves' ears towards the loader. This made them easier to handle. If they were thrown haphazardly one had great difficulty building, and 'G' had a bad habit of going on to the next stook and standing with his fork in the sheaves, ready. By the time the horse stopped and before one could find one's balance, two sheaves would come hurtling up on one's head. Woe betide anyone who let a sheaf fall back to the ground, or part of a load slip off on the way home.

The fields always looked pretty with patterns of shocks running like lines of dots in the distance, decreasing squares to the centre, always following the field slope. These same fields looked so strangely

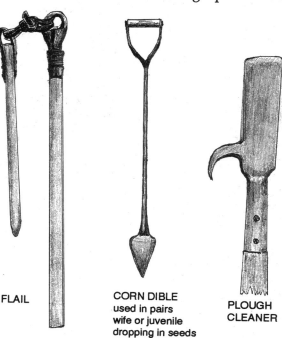

FLAIL

CORN DIBLE
used in pairs
wife or juvenile
dropping in seeds

PLOUGH
CLEANER

empty once the corn was all carted. Guesses would be made at the crop yield and it was surprising how accurate these could be just by judging the density and size of corn. With no spraying, of course, much corn was lost through the suffocation of weeds which invariably shell out during harvest. 'One year's seeding, six years' weeding' they used to say.

It was with some relief harvest was over and the last sheaf thrown very high with 'That's the one we've been looking for.' A series of 'Hear, hear' would be voiced, for though a hard task was finished it was one of several that had to be completed before winter.

> Red of the sun, mist in the hollow,
> Would it be joy, would it be sorrow,
> Stooping man, unlike his straight furrow,
> Who looks at the day, but thinks of the morrow.
>
> Silent, silent are his days,
> Taciturn in many ways,
> The knowing eye looks weather ways
> Short are the nights and long the days.
>
> The last sheaf home, high would fling,
> And thank the Lord for everything,
> With more relief than joy would sing
> All is safely gathered in.

Walking The Hills

As in summer, during harvest we would have many walks over the hills; 'G' would usually go for a good walk after Chapel, for being a good Methodist, 'G' would only do essential work on Sundays and epitomise this by saying 'Harvest never did spoil by not working Sunday.'

The bells of St. Nicholas
Whose chimes fill the air
And the ears of the people
Who are worshipping there.

Grass machines, rotovators,
Pistons that sound,
But the bells of St. Nicholas
Will deaden the sound.

By the old 'pound pond'
In groups or in pair,
For the bells of St. Nicholas
Are calling him there.

The bells are a-ringing
And heard all around,
For it's part of the country's
Sunday sound.

Don't walk in despair
With eyes on the ground,
Hear the bells of St. Nicholas
And follow the sound.

Walk in the great building
Lay your soul bare
In the church of St. Nicholas
And kneel there in prayer.

Church End.

Walking by the church of St. Nicholas and the gravestones of those long since gone, our spirits would rise at the sight of the distant hills, and we would soon be running in front some distance and wait at the foot of 'Stair Way'. This is a path cut in the side of the hill, now averaging about five feet in width, cut from the bottom, slanting to the top, made in all probability by the earliest men who dwelt in these hills, perhaps to help them carry water to their hilltop dwellings or to drive their cattle down to slake their thirst. The pack ponies would have taken a more westerly route up the Old Road in those days as, apart from a few bushes at the bottom end, the rest of the path was clear with just the odd small hazel bush. A grand view was enjoyed whilst climbing and the aged could, with a few rests, climb to the very top and decide which way, east or west, to walk down. If the easterly route was taken a grand vista opened miles to the north, the Bedfordshire plane of gault clay, miles of fields of every colour, from golden stubble and the still green meadows, dotted with grazing beasts, elms, and hedgerows merging on the horizon, or partly hidden in a blue mist. Re-fuelled with a sweet each from 'G', the next step would be the Sand Pits where Mr Gutteridge used to draw out sand for the roads with his horse and cart. By lying down on one's stomach it was just possible to reach the small holes the sand martins made, and by digging down with a stick perhaps the white eggs could be found, though usually they were too far in and out of reach. A couple of hundred yards farther on were the gravel pits. We always probed in these for fossils, which of course we knew little or nothing about. Often there were geologists also looking in the flints and sand for the fossils, often finding bivalves and belemnites of the Jurassic period, for instance. It is odd that glacial and climatic changes millions of years ago brought about such a variety of geological ingredients – chalk, sand and gravel pits all in about a quarter mile radius.

> Any day you have the time
> To stare,
> Find things you never knew
> Were there.

Ravensburgh could be seen on the brow of the hill, a hill fort of some twenty odd acres with encircling ramparts high on the escarpments, some two thousand years old, perhaps much older. The way of life that must have been here makes the mind run riot.

> Brave warriors their dead they laid
> On a high hill
> In a chalk filled grave.
> Their exploits and battles praised,
> And caused a barrow to be raised.

One can visualise rows of men with antler picks scratching down the thin soil overlaying the chalk, forming the lynchets that are there to this day. Some meagre harvest it must have been, and a testimony to their diligence.

Over to the right 'Windy Hole' and the left 'Waiting Hill', where now grow the high Douglas firs and slender beeches spreading and groping with their roots over the chalk for nourishment and minerals. The quiet magic of these woods could sometimes either make the lonely feel afraid or content. At the rear the Cockpits, where a pheasant, the great ventriloquist, threw its voice to be answered by another, and yet another, making a cacophony of sound warning of distant thunder. Artefacts hidden under the searching roots constituted the history of yesteryear, and what better markers could be desired than tall, smooth beeeches, elegant with the light playing in the mosaic of twisted branches like changing Cathedral windows. No Roman or Grecian colonnade could match for beauty these wind-smooth trunks standing in carpets splashed with blue violets, edged with white anemones. Perhaps the quiet cloisters of our ancient cathedrals are the nearest imitations of these great stands of our tallest beechwoods; these only can match the beauty that ascends into the harmonious winds and upwards.

> The chieftain in the earth they laid,
> The grave was filled,
>   The capstone laid,
> His vessel filled
>   With fruits and seeds
> To satisfy his journey's needs.

> O'er runnelled hills
> The mourners' cries
> Make the grey wolves' bristles rise.
> The rutting red deer
> Stays its leap.
> A sad-eyed dog
> Frets in a one-eyed sleep.

It was always with reluctance that one came down into the Hexton fields; perhaps another sweet would help? A mournful yellow hammer would ring over and over 'A little bit of bread and no cheese'. Sheep lay sheltered on the lynchets, and were watched by a kestrel hovering on winnowing wings, high over her russet red eggs lodged precariously on the black twigs of

Old Cottages, Sharpenhoe Road.

her nest. The first of the young rabbits, too young to be aware of danger, jumped fearlessly to and fro from the warrens in the hillside. Waves of sheaves not yet shocked in lines over the sidelands, chequered over 'Braid-Shot'. Hares lolloped over the now-cleared ground, bewildered, conserving their energies for the night. Wild thyme and sweet briar, the red flush of the setting sun over Sharpenhoe Clappers (another hill fort) now rising blue in the distance. Down through the elders and whitethorn in the cut. Sand Pit Road, rough with cart ruts overhung in places where a dove noiselessly flies from its meagre nest, and now in the open, over the road to cut down through Blakelands into the meadow, a chat with the horses and then into the orchard examining the apples. Perhaps this year the Peasgood Nonesuch would be extra large, if so they would certainly be prize exhibits at the harvest festival. Windsor pears would be on the ground being pecked by the hens and and eaten by wasps. Some of the old names of the apples in the orchard I still remember, the well-known Cox's Orange Pippin, and of course Blenheims, Striped Beaufins,

Allington Pippin, Lane's Prince Albert, Wealthy, Winter Green and a Red Victoria, which was a magnificent bright red and an excellent cooker, but one of the sourest apples ever. How often when with a few boys one would look longingly at them. I would say 'You can have all you can eat', one bite would usually suffice. There were other unknown types, of course, and of the pears I remember Windsors, Williams, Jargonals, Louise Bonn. Plums were Victoria, Greengate, Rivers Early Orleans and a small plum we always called Harvest Plum.

The grand Sunday tour is really over. A brief conversation with 'Sarge' on the way home, perhaps two miles covered, everyone in their Sunday best and no sign of anyone working in fields or gardens, and no cattle broken out, for when they do it's usually a Sunday, something I haven't been able to fathom as yet. Farmers then, much like those of today, put their life's blood and love into the sometimes unrewarding soil; part them from that life and they would feel awkward and miserable and yearn to be back to the sometimes driving life that they have always known.

Autumn Gold

Autumn comes in quietly as always, a beautiful time of the year, signifying rest at least to the farmer, with the days shortening, the trees changing from their greens to yellows and golds, merging hues. Even the days seem to languish, content to become shorter. The high clouds in grey rolls sit stationary in the sky, seeming never to want to move or to leave the placidity of the day. Walking to school, kicking the multi-coloured leaves, almost knee deep where they had drifted, and after school with our trucks in a quiet evening, we had to collect the leaves wherever the cooling winds had rustled and drifted them; perhaps offering an added bonus of a little horse manure, for many boys collected leaves and manure to be dug into their gardens or their fathers' allotments. On a dull evening the air is pregnant with a stillness, smoke from the twitch fires that cover the distances in a blue haze overhung with the orange horse-chestnut leaves in lofty branches, unknowingly near to sleep. Swollen Blenheim apples drop with a clonk on the hovel roofs. Ragged rooks lift in the wind, and with the wind blow away to join the straggling line of rooks that stream westward to their Woburn roosts. A few boys stay late and play 'Conkers'; some finish up hanging in the telegraph wires by their string, where they blow like clockwork pendulums for weeks.

The girls finding a late dandelion seedling would pluck it tenderly, blowing away the seeds like tiny parachutes counting the time; or wafting them from the stems would say, 'He loves me, he loves me not' and in the wind they would gently float away. Oil lamps are lit one by one, blinking, and as their glasses warm, are turned up fully to give a glorious inviting warmth through the lead lighted windows, slotting glow patterns outwards, disappearing in the shadows, giving a welcome for the heavy-booted menfolk. Those drowsy, dull days of autumn, falling leaves like golden snowflakes twist downwards, drop noiselessly; in the distance the sound of guns, the pheasants dropping after their first flight of urgency, and on the dry road a chestnut leaf blows, scratching crablike over the tarmac, drifting in a russet pile. In the backdrop the pied magpie rises like an unleashed kite to a loftier perch, fierce-eyed and beneath in the tangle, the small ever-watchful birds jerk-headed, alert for the awesome insatiable cats, so many millions end their life this way every year. The incomprehensibility of keeping a cat and a bird table.

> Jackdaws roost in ruined spire,
> Evening sun sets clouds on fire,
> Geraniumed windows, pools of light,
> Blackbirds in the coppice, sit the night.
> The barking dog lies stilled instead
> To breathe the quiet, for little ones in bed.

The school was closed for a week each year ('tatering') which were bouted out, the bouter like a double-moulded board plough was pulled by two horses running straight down the row, splitting the ridge of potatoes down the middle. This necessitated much kicking with the feet to uncover many of them. Some pickers kicked and others didn't bother too much, which led to many complaints as to who did the job properly. The field would be dotted with people of various sizes, colours and ages, children with toys and children without, women with their backsides turned skywards, some small, some large; some worked hard, while others slacked. The first two or three days were the worst, a back-breaking, earth-drawing job; some who were friends when they first came into the field, were bitter enemies by the time they left.

Workers were paid hourly and the good workers rightly insisted they were working harder than the others. In the end the field would have to be paced and sticks placed at equal intervals, so that everyone was responsible for an allotted length of field. Many long-standing friendships were inevitably lost, and sticks often moved. 'G' always grew King Edwards which were reckoned to be the best grown on the heavy valley fields which reached from Sharpenhoe to Shillington, while Majestic potatoes were considered a lazy man's potato for they were easier to grow and most grew larger in size than Edwards.

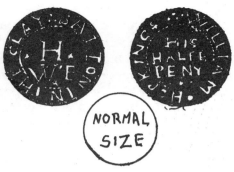

Barton Token.

The temperament of the children varied considerably especially if cold winds blew, or even in early snow, and their dirty little noses would run correspondingly. A few determined not to see it through would howl most of the day, and even the sight of the horses would be enough to send them into fresh tear-gushing outbursts. Frantic mums would push perambulators, their wheels clogged with mud, up and down the field; the jolting alone would be enough for fresh outbursts. Perhaps the youngest would need a nappy change, or to be held out. At the end of the day a bucketful could be taken home, but of course some filled their prams with babies and potatoes. I know of one person who was so bogged down in the mud with her heavy load she asked the farmer to help pull it out. 'You pull the bugger out yourself' he said. 'You're taking more home than me!' He said 'I grow corn and potatoes, but find "crisps" and "corn flakes" too expensive to purchase'.

> The leaves before
> The winter's cold
> Change their cloak
> To one of gold.
> Just ahead of nearing night,
> Each Chiltern valley
> Is a different light,
> Has a separate secret
> Through the night.

The hedgehog
  With its pointed head,
Twisting up
  A thickening bed.
Dead grasses,
  Leaf and fern
Always in
  A forward turn.
So none shall stick
  Upon its quills,
His wreath like
  Winters home he fills.

Six months' toil in an acre of mangolds would near its end in the autumn when rows of Globe and Red Intermediates were pulled, thrown in heaps with their tops cut off in one skilful movement. One was lucky to get through this operation without a nasty cut on the fingers. If there were any extra large ones, perhaps where an old muck heap had stood or some chaff burnt, 'G' would start on these first with great elation. On one occasion he did this, and the cows broke out; they sorted out the largest ones in the field – why or how I never knew – but they ate the lot. I told him they knew, as he did, which were best.

In those days many men were ruptured and couldn't afford time off for the operation. I remember 'G's' belt hanging on the chair back many a time, though he had to be repaired in the end. Hanging on the chair back it looked a very grisly object and was quickly removed at the first sign of a visitor. He also had other troubles, and in bouts of severe pain would wander off and lie down in the field somewhere, writhing in agony, much to the astonishment of any hired help who may have been there. On one of his queer days one had to tread carefully for he would be easily upset. He would soon recover, and though subdued, would soon be back on his own rare form. After his hernia operation he developed other complicated illnesses which increased in intensity until he once more became a patient in the Luton & Dunstable Hospital, this time to have a stone removed from his urinary tract; and, as he put it, tapping his chest, the old ticker was suspect. Unfortunately, the surgeon who removed the stone became friendly with his patient and gave him the stone in a small bottle, which he carried in his waistcoat pocket for years and he would, with the slightest pretext, produce it and tell the tale of how he nearly slipped though their hands, and how the stone was slowly getting smaller and had diminished to half its original size. I have often wondered at the ending of it; perhaps it wore itself completely away.

Forays and Catches

Raids were made into the apple orchards about this time; scrumping they called it, but it didn't worry me overmuch for I hardly ever ate apples, having more than enough in our own orchard where the pigsties, hovels, huts and stables were, forming our base on many occasions when raids were prepared in straw houses, fortresses made with sacks and wood; the huge chaff sacks were very handy for this, covering large areas, though we were expected to put them all back tidy when we had finished. Later when some of the stored apples in the lofts had gone bad, we used to have an aerial bombardment with them, always getting into trouble for this as the rotten apples hurled with gusto used to splatter over the walls of the buildings and hang there for weeks. 'G' was not amused.

'G' purchased an army hut after the 1918 war with a wooden bottom; apples were stored in this on straw, in large heaps. The rats had a great time in the winter, messing and gnawing them, but they were sold nevertheless – the best being picked out and some slightly cleaned. Old Floss the dog would sleep in there but wouldn't take the slightest notice of them on her own, but we used to go up there late evening with torches, stuff some of the rat holes up quickly, and she would tear round in a frenzy until they were caught or had escaped.

The cream of our nocturnal raids were of course walnuts. We would throw cudgels* up at them in the moonlight and grope for them on our hands and knees. If cows were the residents of that particular field, groping hands would find less savoury objects. The walnuts still retaining their green husks left a distinct walnut stain on the fingers, which was, of course, a dead give-away. Fresh walnuts are almost unobtainable in the area now, and instead of sixpence a pound, will soon be 6p each. Very few such trees are left in the village and those that are, are more or less left to beautify with their majestic grey trunks and outstanding bark.

Autumn meant getting down the blackberry hook and searching the hedgerows for the largest, ripest blackberries. Fingers and mouths would soon show a purple staining, for it was difficult for some to put the berries in the baskets and not the mouth. We would hurry in front to find a well-covered bush and say, 'No thieves in my bed'. This gave one an unwritten right to have them all for oneself. If we could gather a nice few, 'G' would sell them on his round in Luton for us. A few bob always came in handy, considering we only had 1d each per week to spend.

Blackberry Blossom.

> Fox makes fur and feathers fly.
> Hawk that hovers in the sky.
> Brooding owls their owlets fed.
> No thieves in my bed.

As the evenings grew darker a few lads would always be out sparrow clapping. This sport was made possible by the boys holding long slender poles with a fine net attached from one to the other, near the top of the poles. The net was about six feet by four feet; the idea was for the net to be held aloft while on the other side if a sparrow's roost was set upon by one or two other boys, with sticks and long poles, when the sparrows flew out into the net, the two lads clapped together the two poles, trapping the birds, and quickly throwing the net down, would take out the birds. Many of these sparrows were taken home for sparrow pie, though by the time I was old enough to partake in this macabre sport, they were taken home for the cats or just counted and left.

In front of our kitchen window was a large ivy arbour, probably erected to make the kitchen window obscure from the Manor opposite. It was about sixteen feet in length and eight feet high, and was the favourite spot for the sparrow clappers, and made perfect cover for the robins each year to raise their young, as did the inch gap between chimney stack and the house where the bats lived. Thatch and corn ricks were another favourite spot for the catchers to murder a few more birds, though owners of thatched houses began to take offence at the probing of their thatch, and it became banned. They used to say 'you do more damage than the sparrows with your poles and zest'.

A time of excitement came round annually; it was a day for rabbiting. A man with a box of ferrets would come for a day's sport to catch the odd rabbit or two. After being starved overnight they were reckoned to be ready for work, and the man would take them out of their little box, fix the collar on the line-ferret and throw the loose one down near the rabbit's hole. Bolt holes would be netted first, and as little noise as possible made, so that the rabbit bolted well. One or two crack shots would stand either side of the hedgerow, and suddenly a rabbit would streak for safety, and if not caught in the net first, would break cover and after a crack of the gun a rabbit could be legged and hung on the hedge to pick up later. Most of the farmers had their own warrens, usually an old moggy tree in the centre of a meadow with plenty of bushes and any old piece of wood thrown against it. Sometimes the rabbit would run up the inside of the hollow tree and the keen ear of the ferret man would locate approximately the whereabouts of rabbit and ferret. An axe would be sent for and a hole chopped in the side of the tree. With any luck the rabbit would be pulled out, with the ferret still hanging on. Many trees still bear this scar to this day. At other times they would perhaps run down the hollow roots and had to be chopped out, or down a dead end hole where they would be 'arsed' up with the ferret, and if not speedily dug out, the ferret would have its fill and be of little use afterwards for chasing. If they were well down in the dark catacombs their whereabouts were followed by pressing the ear to the ground. The line-ferret would then be put down the burrow and when the line became too tight to pull back, it was assumed he had found the lost rabbit and ferret. By sometimes-arduous digging, the line could be followed through a mirage of turns, and sometimes we had to dig tiny holes, the distance to dig being deduced by knots on the line, one knot for a yard, two for two yards, etc. etc. On occasions the line would be almost played out, but, by quiet being observed and with an ear to the ground, short cuts could be made. Great care had to be exercised when the grafter* broke through into the hole, for both rabbit and ferret could be there together.

It took a matter of seconds for a practised man to leg a rabbit, by cutting through the rear of the thigh on the hind leg between the muscle and sinew, pushing the other one through; by snicking the back of the heel it would stop the leg sliding out and the rabbit could then be hung to stiffen on a twig or fence. Great concern was shown by the ferret man when it was found that his cap, which had plugged up a hole, had been filled in and forgotten at the last warren. Jokes were made about the rabbit that ran through the legs of the man with a gun, who, since he had removed the cartridges at the last move, hung helplessly on the triggers with no effect while everyone waited for the rabbit's quick end. Everyone was forced to watch it run, tail bobbing white, to the next retreat, but the rabbit never bolted the second time as easily.

I remember losing a polecat, down in the meadow by the brook, for a fortnight, but I took down the hutch and placed a saucer of milk in it each evening. Imagine my delight in going down one morning and finding it fast asleep in the straw. I always had it on my shoulder whilst cleaning it out, but on one occasion it had the impertinence to bite right through the lobe of my ear. The same ferret had the skin of its jaw ripped by a rat right round its face, but old Floss the dog would sit patiently at the rear of the sheds waiting for the rat to run. If the ferret came out where she sat, it would crawl over her and go back to work again.

Ploughing and Thrashing

Crisp cold days became more regular, fields, hedgerows and allotments would be made tidy, cattle yards cleaned out, manure clamped to rot. One man I heard 'G' talk of walked several miles to work on a farm all day and, in doing so, had to pass a few hundred yards from his allotment, so would walk down there and relieve himself. He really believed in wasting nothing.

> Frosted air when twitch fires
> Spread their smoke
> O'er water, meadows, blankets spread
> Through the stilled woods,
> Smoke clouds grope,
> Make ringlets where the gravestones
> Tell of dead.

We always knew when the ploughing engines were near, for their whistles sounded for miles in the quiet countryside. One could hardly wait for them to come on their yearly visit to plough up Dunstall fields. One would move at the bottom of the field and the other along the hedge by Manor Road, pulling the great ploughs up and down the field with mould boards set either way in a sort of V shape, and they would tip at the ends and be pulled to and fro on their wire ropes. Great was the thrill when one had a ride on these huge wheeled machines, travelling a few yards at a time along the headlands, the great winches turning effortlessly, the steam pressured pistons moving accurately and sliding over their well oiled beds, blackened hands controlling the massive power units with ease and a certain amount of skilled showmanship; the whistle would be blown when the return trip up the field was ready, for a large rise in the field would make one engine invisible from the other. A caravan was pulled from one remote farm to the next, pitched behind one of the engines; when Dunstall was ploughed the caravan was left by the roadside. I used to love going in there in the evening and talking to the engine drivers. They had a little coal stove and small oil lamp. With hands still grimy, they would have a fry up, and cut large hunks of cheese with a sharp knife, which were popped into their mouths with almost the same movement. Even the bunks looked cosier than the nice clean beds that were at home, and it was with great reluctance that I had to leave.

When I was young the Thrashing Machine was a thing to be followed after school. The noise, dust, rats and mice gave a different impression to the one which was held later, when it meant panic, work and dust. When it came it was usual to do most of the farms in the village, one after the other, and was always called the sheene*. Extra help of course was needed. The engine driver looked after the machine and kept it running; he usually had a mate who fed the corn in a well regulated manner into the drum, at least two men on the corn rick, three on straw, one taking corn off in sacks, and one who usually lived rough and didn't mind working in chaff and cavings, the very worst job of the lot. Pensioners were enlisted who didn't really want the job, but they were glad of the money, and they would say, 'I'll give you a hand if you can't get anyone else'. Towards the end of the thrashing era this became very difficult, the old hands dying off and the younger ones being more independent. This was offset a little by someone from another farm helping out his neighbour. Most of the rickyards had been in use for years, and the constant churning of the huge wheels with the biters on, in the rotted straw, made them quagmires and the task of setting the drum in the right position on such an unsuitable bottom became a formidable and very skilled task. As children we loved to watch all this and to be there when the thatch was pulled off, as the expectancy of cracking a rat on the head with a fallen spit filled one with excited anticipation. Boys were kept off the ricks, if possible away from the fork tines, so they stood in a ring round the depleting corn rick, each with a stick to kill all the mice they could. A good dog was necessary for the rats, which were usually in the roof where corn was less depressed, or in holes at the bottom. I remember our old half-bred labrador who had pups in the 'chaff house' when the sheene* came, she followed the sheenes round the farm eating the mice and returning to her pups and regurgitating them. I shovelled up one heap and, flicking them off with a fork, counted ninety-eight.

Once the rick was low enough one could see each sheaf lifted; the little brown furry things would sit huddled in their labyrinth of uncovered tunnels, their beady eyes shining in the unaccustomed light. Balls of shredded straw would roll off the sheaves and tiny pink youngsters with large black eyes, showing through still blind eyelids, would fall squirming for some hungry dog to swallow. I have seen hawks sit on fence posts waiting for stray mice to work their way through the grass.

I remember the unmistakable beat of the drum rising and falling as each sheaf is beaten through the beaters, delicately set so that all the corn was thrashed without cracking too much, and the straw not too mangled; the dust was unbelievable, and of course sacking up the cavings, which were bagged in large chaff sacks, usually full of large holes, was the very ultimate in dust, blown like shot in the face. Chaff cutters would catch the cut and bag the straw, which was emptied into the chaff house adjoining the stables for the horses; the blow chaff was bagged for the cows, to mix with mangolds and cow cake; this was really the sheath that covered each kernel of wheat, the husk, the covering for oats, was the flight. Barley of course had no covering, but was protected with the hale, and terrible things they were too, if one was ever unfortunate enough to get one in the mouth or eye, for though smooth enough in one direction, the other contained scores of minute barbs, and like saw blades would slide smooth in only one direction. If a 'Chaff Cutter' was required, this was placed first at the far end of the drum, for the engine driver would not wish to realign his engine to move it. A very strong horse was needed to shift it in a position under the drum to catch the straw, but old 'Bonny' would dig in her toes and with the help of all hands on the wheels would manage it. Oats were then cut into chaff with huge shaped blades and blown into huge bags, called chaff sacks, which were then taken up to the stable loft, shaken out over a planked wall to fill the whole area; as children we had the dusty job of spreading and treading it down. Later when the chaff was mostly used we had great fun jumping about twenty feet down on to its soft surface.

'G' kept his apiary at the bottom end of the Orchard called the garden, which was filled with fruit trees and still had roses, daffodils and snowdrops growing more or less wild. Mostly as children we kept well clear of them, apart from the occasional pruggle and quick run with the bees in pursuit. 'G' kept an old hoe blade and a piece of chaff cutter knife, so, faced with the likelihood of them swarming, one of us had to ring together the pieces of iron, which was supposed to create swarming preferences through the sound waves created. Whether or not this method of keeping one's swarm was ever effective I never knew, but I do remember seeing some swarms disappear quickly over the elm stalms, some hung fascinatingly, some very bulbous, others tapered like Roman amphora. Any news of swarms in the village would soon be passed on by his friends, and if they were any good, and early enough, 'G' would go for them. He rarely wore a veil or gloves, and would wade into an air filled with bees, and shake them into his straw hives, leave them on the ground with a stone under one side for the rest to follow the queen, and pick them up with a piece of cloth underneath tied at the top, in the cool of the evening. We would watch with fascination when in the autumn he would 'take them up' to get the honey. The first year I remember he left them in the round straw hives; before this time the Manor was two separate houses and I understand bee hives were made at one of them, so that some of 'G's' hives would have been made there. With rolled corrugated brown paper he would put it in a special container and light it, and while it smouldered, with the bellows on the side he would puff the smoke into the hive to stupefy the bees. Taking up the whole of the hive and honey, he would bring it home, where we would look fascinated at the rows of comb and the little hexagonal cells sealed and filled with honey. He would ladle a sticky morass on a plate for us to suck. Before honey separators were available, 'G' used to ladle out the honey into a large cloth, tie the ends together and hand them on a pole between two chairbacks, and catch the honey in a basin underneath; what he didn't give away he sold for about 1/- (5p) a jar.

I only remember 'G' being stung once. He had one hive of particularly nasty bees, which I think must have been wild, for they had their armed scouts out in an almost solid ring of patrol; anyone venturing within sixty or seventy yards of their hive would be stung. The day 'G' said he would examine them we waited with baited breath. 'They won't sting me', he said with experienced confidence, but he hadn't been many seconds before he said 'Durnit, boy, they have'. His confidence was visibly shattered. They stung him several times on the arms. I've never once heard him swear, though there were times when he said if things were going bad, 'it's enough to make a

The Burr family making beehives at the now-called 'Manor House'.

saint swear'. He, like all those of his time, left school at the age of eleven, but was self-taught enough to express himself without the use of violent words.

Although 'G' was tactless, outspoken and tended to find fault in others, he also knew his own faults, and would help anyone, given the chance, and though never wealthy, supported charities. I believe a cot is named after him in the Children's Home at Harpenden. If people lived as he did, simply, that others may live, the world would be easier to live in. There is a tendency today to worship what a man has achieved moneywise for himself, rather than to help others.

> Look up to the man
> > Who with luck has grown rich.
> Look down on his poorer brother,
> > For a man is a fool
> To work hard they say,
> Or stay to help another.

There was a time when a neighbour was a bit short on horses for harvest; 'G' had not always seen eye to eye with him, but when the last sheaf was home 'G' asked him if he would like to have a horse and cart to help out, an offer which was readily accepted. One day the horse was left with a load of corn and she must have felt a little homesick, for she turned round in the yard, and brought the load of corn all the way home intact. Those who know how a horse had to be guided out by gateposts, so that the hubs of the cart missed the posts as the horse turned, will know that this was no small piece of navigation.

When a smallholder who lived up by the Church wanted some cats, 'G' soon found him some. The trouble was, I had to carry them, and as they were surplus to the mill owner's requirements, I had to carry them in a sack from one end of the village to the other. They were almost wild and full grown, but not as wild as I was, for I just couldn't keep their claws out of my backside. I swear they weighed as much as two full grown dogs by the time I had them at their destination.

Village view.

Each Saturday evening my sister and I would go down the lane in the darkness to spend our weekly 1d and also purchase the evening paper with its football results, for 'G'. The hedgerows were overgrown and high, and there were no houses from the corner near the Manor until one reached the main road, they themselves being surrounded by trees. Halfway down on the right behind a row of wych elms the gypsies were always camped. The lights from the fires could be seen leaping behind the hedgerow, making large and very dark shadows change in to strange shapes. We would clutch our penny tightly and quicken our pace, for we were, in the language of our day, plain frit*. We would spend some time looking in the shop windows, undecided on how best to spend our penny, if to split it in half and purchase two articles for a halfpenny each, or have a grand slam and spend the whole lot at once. We used to look in 'Pecks' shop, one window had the pennies in and the other two pennies; longingly we used to gaze at the tuppence worth but always going back to the cheap window. 'G' didn't like us spending our weekly penny there; I think it was because Mrs Peck was a Baptist, 'G' of course being a Methodist. The Baptists didn't like the Catholics, and so on.

We knew it would be no good getting too much for our money, as the sweets had to be handed round when we returned, and 'G' would be first to say 'you've got some cheap old things here', so it became a major decision deciding on what suckers* would suit all. 'G' also had a preference on which shop we gave our regular custom to, so consideration had to be taken over that as well, so that it was no small thing even to spend a penny. Top level decisions had to be taken weekly and some of the sweets left over for the Sabbath. One slightly unsavoury character would sit in a grocery shop on a stool gossiping and squirting spit on the floor, much to everyone's disgust.

Trips to the Luton Mission were taken by bus on some Saturday evenings, and on very special occasions 'G' would take us all in with him to the Celebrity Concerts which were held there. Leading concert artists came and this was my first introduction to serious music, and I think what struck me most was the long, disciplined quiet during intervals, and one's behaviour had to be at its peak to sit through an hour and half with hardly a wriggle. I knew the singing must be good and tried to discipline my mind to concentrate on the long solos in

High Street.

their entirety, but found the violin the hardest to accustom my ears to. One evening I shall never forget was when 'Sarge' decided to meet us in our usual seats up in the gallery. He had some shopping to do, so arrived late, tiptoed in and took his seat. Halfway through the concert during an intermission when a pin could be heard to drop, his alarm clock, which he had purchased unbeknown to us, suddenly went off with a terrible loud ring. 'Sarge's' face became redder and redder, and the people on the left looked right, and the ones on the right looked left, the heads of people below looked upwards. 'Sarge' lifted up his leg with the heel hovering threateningly; just then it stopped as suddenly as it started. Relief was evident and stifled amusement easy to discern. Just as things were becoming normal, off it went again, it was a repeater. I'm sure it must have been his most embarrassing moment!

Horses and Hunts

Trips to the farrier were exciting and took place during the slacker times, if that could be arranged. The Hexton smithy closed, leaving the nearest at Streatley, a Mr G Kingham, renowned for his skill and knowledge of horses; with his sweat band and handkerchief tied on his head, leather apron and slightly protruding eyes, his forehead always bathed in sweat, he would lean on the bellows, pumping them with his forearm while drinking thick cocoa from a very large and grimy jug with the other. He would talk to 'G' about women, corn, and horses' feet – mostly about horses' feet. His red First Prize tickets stuck over much of the shop along with the winning shoes. He would wade skilfully through piles of miscellaneous objects, heaps of old shoes, lengths of iron. If I could make up his fire, or puff with his bellows, it made my day. When the horse was taken in he would walk in front, booting away all the loose objects on the floor, old shoes, files, rasps and curved pieces of hoof. He would alarm me by swearing in front of 'G', hitting the horse's ribs with his rasp or any other object he had in his hand including his hammer, but the shaping of the red hot shoes on his anvil had to be seen to be believed, and the tapping of the hammer on the anvil, while his scrutinising eyes critically looked first one side and then the other, kept a steady fascinating rhythm.

> Rain runs gutterwise
>   from eaves,
> Wind furls through
>   the autumn leaves,
> Rose dappled apples loose
>   their winter fare,
> Suspicious hens crane their
>   necks and stare.

One of the mares we kept, Jenny, had only one fault and that was her bad feet. Great pieces broke from them and to keep shoes on her for any length of time was a great tribute to him. Each nail had to be driven in her shoes with precision. Sometimes he would bend them carefully to ensure their precise entry into the hoof, and on these occasions would show his true skill and gentleness. Though he hated seeing her and it would make him swear to see her coming, in the end he solved the problem once again by telling us to let her go without being shod at all, and just trim up her feet with a rasp and they would become hardened; he was of course right. At harvest time nose-bags would be hung on the horses' heads, and they developed the knack of tossing their heads back, to shake the oats upwards, which being heavier always sank to the bottom of the chaff. It was much like the young girls seen on the 'telly' today, who continually and habitually do the same, to throw their hair out of the eyes. But unlike horses who were groomed, currycombed, brushed, polished, their tails tied with straw, before they were even allowed to go in perhaps the next field, to plough all day.

When I was old enough to take a horse on my own, it was a great day. 'G' purchased a horse bred at Newmarket but too heavy for racing. He was a beautiful dapple grey, tall and strong, and could pull a two-horse roll all day, almost at running pace. His name was Joe. 'G' would throw a sack on his back and say, 'Take him to Streatley, you can trot him a little'. I would guide him to the hedgerow, break off a little twitchy stick and off we would go, and when he had his new shoes on, one could hear them clonk on the metalled road and I would ride him full gallop down the cutting. The first two horses I remember most were Bonny and Dolly. Bonny was a tallish horse and had been through the 14–18 war and carried the army brand on her shoulder. She would jib at nothing, but to make her hurry was impossible, her hide being so thick she didn't seem to feel the whip, and the only thing to make her hurry was if a gun was fired near her. The tragic way she gained this nervousness didn't sink in until years after her death, and one can only look back now with absolute horror at the terror these animals must have gone through.

Bonny had a foal before 'G' purchased her, and after finding out the merit of her mother, he bought the foal also and called her Dolly, broke her in himself, and I remember her pulling a large apple tree round and round the meadow to get the feel of the pull on the collar. After the introduction of the tractor the horses became redundant and the implements were made to fit the tractor drawbars. After a year or so of doing nothing but graze, they were with some sadness sold, and things became less personal after their going.

> The craftsman's hammer,
>> Well tuned bell,
> Taps a peal
>> I knew so well.
> An anvil chime
>> The ears did fill,
> The reverberations
>> Returning still.

Only vaguely can I remember the Otter Hunt meeting at Barton, when they used to search the reed beds and brooks down Faldo Road, the moated house of Beechener's Farm, and many ponds that were then full. I used to remember the Fox Hunts, and must confess that I enjoy the Meets even now. When we became old enough to run after them, we knew the woods they would drive and the probable route the escaping fox would make and knowing many short cuts were always well up with the field. It seemed so much part of the country environment to see these horses galloping through mud, snorting and puffing, the thundering hooves splashing in pools. One stood well back out of the way, and soon they would be gone, a stream of hounds making distances seem short and some well filled back ends with trim knicker work showing through as though they had been blown in under pressure.

Bedford Road

A look disdain
  With voices rather haughty.
Well-filled jodhpurs
  That look rather naughty.
Running around the same
  Old field all day,
Drive horse and rider
  Insensible they say,

Great endeavour mirth
  To hide,
Of a horse breaking wind
  At every stride,
With petite young ladies
  At the rear,
Pretending hard
  They didn't hear.

The woods looked black after early rain and the riders'
white breeches shone brilliantly, their scarlet coats in the thin
bright winter's sun against the black backcloth, a certain natural
beauty to see them undulating at full gallop when the fox was
away. Not often was one caught, though I remember one being
chased through the village and committing suicide by jumping
over the wall at the rear of the Baptist Chapel and diving
straight into a tank of water – drowning by total immersion I
think they called it. There is much controversy over this sport
now. I know about hunting a poor fox that has perhaps spent
the night killing off a score of hens, for the sheer devilment of it,
or running horses almost insensible round the same hills, and
the haughty scraps of conversation from the waiting field. I
often wonder if these people, who gather at Meets and find
demonstrations both easy and fashionable, give their fellow
creature as much attention. In truth though, the foxhound is a
beautiful placid animal. They hunt in the patches of snow, dead
ferns, black earth in harmonious camouflage, a wonderful
sight. They are kept in kennels now and always numbered in
pairs, often seeing but one man, yet when they tumble out of
their trucks with waves of white-tipped tails wagging, nuzzling
the small children, brushing their velvet ears against them,
looking up with their kind intelligent eyes, saying with them,
perhaps, 'this is but a brief encounter before the chase.'

> So many charitable
> Works to do,
> All the suffering
> Near to you.
> Starvation and all the world
> With dangers fraught
> Forget it all,
> For foxes may be caught.
> Fatality of the human race
> Join the queers
> To stop the chase.

Winter Preparations

Thatching was another task to be completed as soon after harvest as possible. It took too long and was too tedious and exacting for 'G'; before I managed this job he employed someone to do it for him. Straw would be taken to the field and put by the ricks, shaken up as straight as possible and watered down and patted to keep it tight and knock the water well in. By morning it would be tight and damp, and pulling out the protruding ends and releasing them in a line, some nice straight straw would be made ready. A rope was put on the ground and the straw in sort of flat armfuls was laid on it, each one out of line with the one below and each one called a yelm*, and if six were required to run up the length of the roof this was called a stelch*. The rope was tied usually through an old hurdle iron for easiness, carried up the ladder and placed in easy reach on a dung fork stuck well in the roof. Each of the yelms could be taken out, their separation effected by the criss-cross pattern, each one slightly overlapping the other starting at the bottom, spits were stuck in the roof in readiness, and the sack string rolled on short pegs, to follow a line around, lacing down the straw which was gently combed first, tied and clipped at the bottom to give a nice finished appearance. A well-thatched rick with shining straw, clipped level, always looked creditably good and could throw off rain for most of the winter, the chief enemies being rats underneath and rooks on top if the winter was very severe. The sticks driven well in were usually hazel, the thickest being split down and called spits. If the roof didn't overhang enough to throw the water, long bundles tied with straw were tucked under the roof and the thatch run over it. These were called bastards, and the making of these was my first introduction to this country art. I think with the coming of combines to the village, the last ricks to be thatched in Barton

Scotching the wheels at the top of Old Road.
From left to right: J. Peck, C. O'Dell, G. O'Dell and I. O'Dell.

were done by myself, and although I say it 'no one else will', they were a well accomplished piece of workmanship, built, thatched, and trimmed by me with the sure knowledge that whatever the weather the corn would be safe and dry.

> Lashed by the throwing wind,
>   Ash buds knock
> Black rheumatic fingers
>   In ash grey smock.
> An incessant moan
>   Through the great elms rock,
> Where rugged sentinels
>   The high rooks flock.

In preparation for winter the wood which had been standing up against the larger fruit trees would, in any spare time or wet days, be sawn into splittable lengths with a cross cut, split with an axe, and thrown into large piles under the hovel for future use, for Mother careful as always never had a fire to speak of during the day, as it was mainly composed of slack, cabbage leaves and potato peelings. As the time came near for 'G's' homecoming, things had to move a bit for he was always furious to come home to a dull fire. He would come in every evening with a huge sack of split logs and dump them down by the fireside next to his chair, and in between dozing during the evening would throw, or hurl would be a more apt term, five or six logs at a time, so the heat fluctuated between very hot and almost cold. 'I like to hear the paper crackle on the wall,' he used to say, as indeed it often did. Occasionally his aim would misfire sending out a cloud of hot ashes. Mother would 'tut', spring up, do a dance stamping them out before they could burn the rug. His thirst for wood was unsatiated, one could hardly keep up with his demand, for he would not mix coal with his wood; in fact in later years, after I was married, he could burn a day's work in a couple of nights, and to keep enough for myself I had to stoop to the mean trick of hiding some. Mother's low fires were a drawback to me in my younger days, for I was in great trouble if I came home with wet feet, and I invariably did. I would take off my shoes and try in vain to dry my feet by hanging them over the fender as near to the fire as possible, but if I poked or touched the fire, Mother would come in the room, sniff and accuse me of playing with the fire. If 'G' was a little early coming home he would catch Mother on the hop – 'You haven't much of a fire, Ade' he would say, and set about solving the problem.

Winter was never here, we thought, until we saw some snow, and when the first flakes fell, used to look out of the school windows to see if it was settling.

> The first flakes falling softly
>> Curling in a cobbled yard.
> Swirling, rising, and drifting
>> In the corners hard.
> A dull grey blanket was the sky
>> That never passes
> But with the falling
>> And the dancing in the grasses.

A good snow followed by a frost would make sledging possible. Most families had their own sledge, home-made of course. They were never called toboggans, and many never had runners, nothing more than two pieces of wood on the edge and a few pieces nailed flat across the top. The very large ones would hold half a dozen fully grown people and were called family sledges, and if one of these caught you in the back when a bit wet and heavy it was almost fatal. All sledge tracks from the village converged at the Wash Brook meadow, which ran up the hill through a gap in the hedge, and continued to a small Dell west of the Leet Wood which was probably quarried for lime at one time; the kilns were discovered when the water station was installed. If the going was good one could start at the top of the Dell, zoom down, up, and over the ridge and down to the gap in the hedge, which was hard to negotiate if it had turned to ice. If one couldn't make it, one crashed into the whitethorn hedge one side or another. If one could, then terrific speeds were encountered and with the sledge bouncing over the small ridges left over from old cultivations, you shut your eyes and hoped for the best, and before you knew it you had crashed into the wire fence by Wash Brook at the bottom. We had a shorter track through the Linces down Primrose Hill, but the most hair-raising one was when most of the snow had disappeared and Stairway, the narrower track about five or six feet wide lying on the east, retained the snow up to the very last. Brave attempts were made to sledge down the last couple of hundred yards of this ribbon of snow. This proved very dangerous; the sledge would shoot over the side and down the steep part, going much too fast to roll off, the fronts of the sledges would stick into the flat at the bottom, while the occupant shot over the top with a bang and thump onto the frozen earth, jarring every bone in the body.

The hills looked so different covered in snow. Plum Pudding looked like an upturned white pudding basin; in fact all the hills along the the lynchets and medieval plough ridges gave the impression of great white seas, frozen and stilled, dappled only by tiny footlings of pad and claw, mostly pointing to the woodlands which looked dark under the white hillsides, in the windless pockets their branches hang burdened with snow. The rabbits' pad marks were dead give-aways, and a poacher would note which burrows were being used by the traffic marks, also the best place for a snare, where the footlings converged through some narrow opening. The lone pheasant would unwittingly leave the claw marks to tell of its presence and habitat, its scratching clearly seen in the dead leaves where snow was thinnest. Many have been surprised to see that rats have been near to the front doors overnight, leaving their little toe and heel marks and often the thin line of their tails showing the snow. It was like there was no atmosphere on a clear night, bright with frost. The tawny owl wippled eerily and the silvered stars hung as though on webs from the sky, crunchy footsteps left flattened in icy grass, and under the moon a frosting. The crinkle-nosed rabbit, whiskers twitching, snuffles plates of leaves, wafting down forming golden doorways to his warren.

> When the wind blows round the round ricks
> Children deep in dreams are sleeping,
> Shutters bang and rack the loose board,
> Sleeping lovers lock in love arms.

Sometimes a good slide was obtained in the playground if the School Master would allow us to throw water down overnight, but it was more usual to slide on the ponds which were down Faldo Road, one in front of Grange Farm and one by the roadside lower down. There was a very deep one at the rear of 'Manitoba', a small parcel of ground on the right. One popular place to slide was Manor Road down the hill on to and across the main road, something that would be suicidal today.

The Changing Scene

So much has changed in the last sixty or seventy years. The village is now like a small town, and there would be little grass to graze cows in Back Lane. Paddocks and pastures all succumbed to development; instead of one small school we now have four, the largest being built on entirely the wrong spot, a savage monstrosity on the one remaining road of some beauty.

> Let's first have health
> and then have wealth
> or better both together,
> I doubt I'll have either one
> But better late than never.

High Street, Harry Cain's, subsequently replaced by the Co-op.

Before the bypass one could scarcely cross the main road without running, owing to the heavy flow of traffic. It could be almost as quick to shop in Hitchin or Luton about six miles away as it was to park and shop in the village on a Saturday! (We now have a car park.)

High Street. (Now by-passed.)

The horses have returned; instead of Clydesdale and heavy breeds of mixed parentage, they are mostly hacks with smartly attired girls astride them, going to gymkhanas to run round poles and do peculiar things with potatoes.

The thick-legged Golden Plover may return to the arable roof of the hills, but the weird shriek of the otter will never be heard in the Faldo Waters, and the nightingale just could return to some remote outskirts, but it is doubtful.

Perhaps the badger will be found again on the hills, a pair seeking new territories will find the ever-growing cover on the hillsides to their liking and will have better luck than the last two, which remained undetected long enough to dig out a set in the Lead Wood, but were fiendishly dug out by over-zealous keepers.

The melodies of the pitched bells on the necks of sheep will no longer spill their delightful music through the quiet of a Sunday morning, but memories will remain in the minds of a lucky few who can only hope for something equally as beautiful to be born in these scientific, computerised days. Some rural charm, however, still exists but needs to be searched for.

Winter has overtaken us again, and just before dark I had my present-day walk up and over the hills. They are much the same; some of them like White Hill, which we used to climb in a line to kick a ball up, are now unclimbable, with undergrowth and young trees covering their steep sides. The path to riches is still there for those who see.

> The Gainsboroughs and the Turners,
> Painted colours they could see.
> The things they once painted
> Are still there, for you and me.
> Riots of colours, rocks, or plough set fair,
> Go into the country
> You'll find that they're still there.

Up through the sticky clay by the new cemetery over the water where the old bridge once stood, ankle deep in the rustle of horse chestnut leaves, or on the bank side where footlines are half full of water seeping from the higher lands, by what was once called Primrose Hill but is now huge anthills and whitethorn bushes, the elder trees leaning away from their tall neighbours show green moss on their northern sides, for the sun's hours are short here. The drifting wood forms its own dam, soft pools like dogs' eyes, catching a glint of light and reflecting. The strong southwesterlies moan in the Lead Wood like a distant motorway only much more sweet. Scudding clouds of blue and grey toss weakly, like smoke from different fires seeming to rise from the backs of the hills themselves, beaming a kaleidoscope of coloured patches leaping over the curves of the hills and away across far horizons.

By hazelnut coppices bunched with ivy, over the shallow spring water, tinkling over a hard bottom of stones, not quite to the Springs where the hills come suddenly up the grassless slope to the north of Plum Pudding hill, pausing to look over the valley bottom, and hear plainly the sweet sounds of the wind in the highest clump of beeches through their tall vaultings and delicate tracery, northern gatements on the Chiltern escarpments, probably a minor hill fort, or at least a boundary ditch. The high smooth branches stand out like aerials pointing skywards, picking up the music from heaven, the topmost stand loud in the wind and sound like an orchestra playing down through audiences of hazel, ash and fir, rolling down the notes onto vast carpets of Old Man' Beard, or Traveller's Joy, that drape the coppice like huge white blankets, keeping warm the damp valley bottom for the winter months. Perhaps, on an autumn morning, after a good rain in a clean sharp dawn, the trees against the dark woods would still be festooned with rain tears, hanging and shining in large globulets; like a patch of starlit sky, the odd one through refraction, changing lights of red, amber and silver. In the slight movement of air, a rainbow or light tinkles over the cold black branches, a kaleidoscope of beauty, to be lost in the first shudder of the wind.

In the old favourite places the pheasants tell of their roostings, while the sun sinks lower and with the last piercing beam lights up the autumn maple in a rich glow, the grasses quiver in the twilight as the cloak of night descends. Round the north of Plum Pudding, south of the lynchets climbing up the Bronze Age field peri-

Cuckoo Pint or Lords and Ladies.

meters, some perhaps two thousand years old, now indistinct lines of shadows, still climbing to the exhilarating air of the summit and the last northern terraced escarpment. It's now dark, one can just see the rabbit 'tells' on little piles of scratched earth, lovers deep in the hazels hide 'neath the catkins' bowers, oblivious of their give away with little squeals of mirth. The ivy now dark, like old men climbing the wychelms and the last and bottom lynchet. Down in the clay valley the extending rows of street lights tell that Barton is still there and will soon be slumbering. An old man, back bent, with spade and bag of briars once trudged home, satisfied with the shillings he had earned 'briaring'.

Money talks
You've heard the cry.
I heard it once,
It said 'Goodbye'.
Give me the simple things of life
Violets, a growing tree,
A child's smile that lasts awhile.
These things will do for me.

A golden calm in autumn,
Softest winds in spring,
Eyes that know of love,
And good in everything.

These are my paths to riches.
These are my treasures.

Quotes

Barton man hoeing sun-baked clods.
 'Gert old sodders, you can't do nothing widum, mindn't as well drag your tool along the ground.'

Barton woman talking of a nosey person.
 'She wants to know the way to "Megs" arse and how far it is.'

Barton man sees fox running from 'hen-house'.
 'I seed the bloody thing coming out of the "enus"; it guts were full and he warn't arf a big ol' bugger.'

Barton woman talks of local gossiper.
 'She's too much of what the cat licks its arse with.'

Self-explanatory.
 'He's too lazy to stand bow-legged if he sh-t himself.'

Local sizing up another.
 'I've seen plenty of two-faced men in my time but there's a man coming now who 'as a face for everybody.'

Barton man lifting heavy weight.
 'Made my arse pouch so much you could have sliced washers off.'

Barton man over incessant noise.
 'Enough to charm the guts out of a wheelbarrow.'

Barton woman to a hungry child.
 'You're not satisfied full no fasting.'
'G's' very apt quote.
 'The lame and lazy are always provided for.'
He also used to say.
 'A crow should be able to fly through a well layered hedge.'

Barton farmer feeding cattle with inferior feed.
 'It'll all help make a turd.'

At the Local.
 'Has the beer goes down, the spirits rise the corn yields with it.'
 'Thought it had gone out of me head. But found it on the tip of my tongue.'
 'The lark on a high.'
 'A hide bound cow.'
 'She was so fat she could fall either way and do no damage.'

'Run frightened, like a buttend arsed terrier.'
'She got carried away, or she should have been.'
Of a child, smiling seraphically, covered in 'Cadbury'.
'He's a grabber, when he was on the dole he wanted overtime.'

Words fail me –
'Suffering from phraseological inexactitude.'
'Having a love look of a dog.'

'G's' quote.
'Said a neighbouring farmer would never be wealthy, he put his money on the wrong kind of gee-gee.'

Overheard.
'They should be hung then imprisoned for the rest of their lives.'

Modern quote.
'I'm goner put my feet up and my arse down and watch "Telly".'

On barbecues –
'They used to feed inside, go down the garden to the lav', now they have the lav' inside and feed in the garden.'

Two farmers.
'I've never known him lash his money out like that before.'
Second farmer.
'He's certainly split his arse this time.'

Old farmer finding his horse dead.
'He's never done that before.'

Wife, after husband inadvertently broke wind in bed.
'My God, another one like that and I will wake up dead.'

'Bright morning sun
    Rain sure to come.'

Modern Verse

> The 'Do-Gooders' can now be blamed
> For no one's to be slapped or caned.
> Don't open the door
> Or go out alone
> You could be robbed, raped or maimed.

Last Quote
'For what shall it profit a man, if he gain the whole world, and lose his own soul?'

St. Mark. Chapter 8
Verse 36.

*Glossary

ACKIES OUT	Hiding game using tin can for base	BULLACE	Wild plum, blue or yellow
AGIN	Against	BUSTERS	Soft sorbo balls
ALLUS	Always	CART KNOCKING	Well greased cart should knock well whilst travelling
ARRAP	Scratch		
ARSED UP	Rabbits curled tight in end of burrow when pursued by ferret or dog	CAST	Horse stuck fast
		CATTY CUNGLE	Tip Cat game
		CAVINGS & CHAFF	Dirtiest job thrashing
BAIT	Chaff, bran and oats for horses, or workman's lunch	CHAP REIN	For leading horses
		CATY	Catapult
BAMOX	Knock down roughly	CHEER	Chair
BANKING BOLT	Mythical local bird	CHOPS	Cheeks
BEAVER	Mid-morning grub	CLARABOUT	For ever rushing about
BEDFORDSHIRE CLANGER	Meat pudding roll, meat one end, jam the other	CLARING	Tearing about, rushing
BIGUNS	Older children, anything large	CLARTED	Dirty
		CLOMP	Tread heavy
BLARMIT	Blow it	CLOUTER HEAD	Stupid boy or person
BLART	Shout or cow blarting	COCK ROW	First and middle row of hay one either side being placed on to make entire haycock
BODGE	Make do, patch up, half done		
BOUTER	Plough with double mould board for splitting ridges of potatoes	COCK UP	Pheasant
		COME HITHER	Turn horse to left or T'ward
BRAMER	Flighty or over-dressed girl	COPSE & LADDER	Placed on front and rear of cart for extra loading
BRUCK	Broken		
BRUZZY	Thistles or bruzzy headed cabbage with no heart	COTCHEL	Small heap or load of corn

CRANFIELD MAN OR LAWYER	Large logs or posts for supporting bulging corn ricks
CRIB BITER	Horse that bites its manger, etc.
CRUPPER	Used in harness for retaining horse's tail
CRUPPERED	Caught or entangled
DEVILS GUT	Roots of Great Bell bine
DILLUP	Point of balance (stand on the front of load, it's on the dillup)
DISH WASHER	Water wagtail or pied wagtail
DRAR	Drag
DRENCH	Cattle drink medicine
DUFFOUS	Pull end of rick roof in sharp, perhaps through misjudgement
FAGGOT	Bundle of sticks. Pea sticks tied in bundles
FAIR TO MIDDLING	Fair health
FALL BACK ON	Anything saved, always handy to fall back on
FOOTLINS	Foot or pad marks
FORREST HORSE	Leading horse
FORK TINE	Prong of fork
FRIM	Quick growth, unnatural
FRIT	Frightened
FRUZ	Froze
FUST	First
GAWPING	Starting, perhaps open-mouthed

GEE'O	Go to right
GERT	Great
GISOLT	Give us hold
GNAW	Narr
GOLLOPING	Rudely eating
GRAFTER	Long narrow spade
GRAMMER'D UP	Too much clothing for comfort
GUZZLE	Drink fast
HACKLES UP	Dog's bristles up, or one's temper
HAY LOFT	Tallet
HAYSEL	Beginning to dry, soil will soon be workable
HELVE	Axe handle
HEMP HALTER	Bridle made of hemp
HIS'N	For his
HER'N	For hers
HOBOWCHIN	Daddy-long-legs or crane fly
HOSS	Horse
HOVEL	Open shed mostly used for carts
HUNK	Thickish hunk of cheese and bread
HOMMOCKS	Clumsy feet
HURLOCK OR HULLOCK	Hard chalk cores, or lumps
INGUNS	Onions
IPPER	Left side of cart
LITTLE SNOT	Miserable child
LIVERY	Heavy compact soil, hard to move, sad
LOB CART	Fill all carts before returning to empty
LODGED	Corn flattened by rain and wind, lodged together

MOGGY	Cat, or tree lopped and becoming misshapen	SET CART	One cart in field, one on road, and one unloading
MORISH	Good, tasty	SHEP DUG	Sheep dog
MUCKARSING	Playing, wasting time	SHEENE	Thrashing machine
MUGIN	Dull, heavy rain	SHOCKED CORN OR LAID	Corn after a storm, twisted all ways, stacking the shocks
NUT STALM	Nut brush and hazel	SHOCKS	Stooks, sheaves set up in fields to dry for collection
ODGLE	Alter, unable to move, can't odgle it anyhow	SKEGS	Wild plums
OGEE BOY	Boy for leading the horse	SKILLY	Very thin soup
OMMOKS	Trample	SLUDDER	Churned up mud
ONKED	Awkward	SNARTH	Scythe
OTCHEL	Hard to move, sacks of corn otcheled with knees and elbows	SNOTTY WELL	Don't let me snotty-well catch you here again
OX	To send, ox the boy out	SOLDIER	Thistle
		SOLLY	End of bell rope
PITCH HOLE	Hollow in side of rick, man stood to pass up corn	SPALT	Piece of wood that splinters easily
PILL	Stream of cold water from drain	SPARROW CLAPPING	Catching sparrows in nets during darkness
QUARTERNS	Loaf of bread, or women's breasts	SPIT	Sharpened or split stick used for thatching
RAVES	Top board of cart body angled outwards	SPITCHER	A piece of tile used in hopscotch
RIGHT AS A TRIVET	Upstanding, trivet three-legged stand for kettle, etc.	SQUABBER	Slasher for trimming hedgerows
SACK STRING	Binder twine	STALCH OR STELCH	One armful of straw used for thatching
SALLY	Hare		
SCRIBBLING LARK	Yellow hammer, so called owing to egg markings	STALM	Nut stalm, nut brush and hazel
		STANING	Areas of space for horse or cow
SCRUMPING	Stealing apples, a scrump – small wizened apple	STICK & HALF	Flail

STOLSH	Walking in wet conditions, stolshing about	UNPUNDLE	Unpin and tip up cart at point of balance
STUNT	Low angle of roof, house or rick	UVERING	Hovering, wind being uvering, sign of rain
SUCKER	Sweet or toffee		
SUT	Soot	WADDING	See COCK ROW
SWIMMER	Suet dumpling	WANTY	Wide rope band, belly band
SWINGLE BIT	Tool for making straw bands from loose straw rick	WARNT	Want
SWOUNED	Swooned	WATER-BOYS	Small bluish grey clouds, forerunners of rain
SCREWS	Rheumatics		
TAKING OUT	Tying up scythed corn into sheaves	WEATHER BREEDER	An unusually pleasant drying day, forerunner of rain
THECKING	Thatching	WEE-UP	Hullo, or how are you
THE OLD POKER	Affectionate term for shotgun		
THROWING IN	Throwing in sheaves close, handy for shocking up	WELL TIMBERED	Good strong legs, sometimes describing a girl
		WESSCOT	Waistcoat
TOE RAG	Worn by older men before socks, sometimes used as a term of abuse	WHIPPLE -TREE	Wooden separators for means of pulling by chains from horse's collar to implement
TRAFFIC	Runs made by vermin, or mud left by their feet	WUSS	Worse
		YOUR'N	Yours
TRAIPSE	Anything walking about with muddy feet		
TROMPING	Like traipsing, perhaps in a heavier way		
TWIZZED	Wrapped around, tangled		
UBBER	Right hand side of cart		
UGTROUGH	Pig trough		
UNKED	Loutish, uncouth		

Books Published by THE BOOK CASTLE

JOURNEYS INTO HERTFORDSHIRE: Anthony Mackay.
Foreword by The Marquess of Salisbury, Hatfield House.
Nearly 200 superbly detailed ink drawings depict the towns, buildings
and landscape of this still predominantly rural county.

JOURNEYS INTO BEDFORDSHIRE: Anthony Mackay.
Foreword by The Marquess of Tavistock, Woburn Abbey.
A lavish book of over 150 evocative ink drawings.

**COUNTRYSIDE CYCLING IN BEDFORDSHIRE,
BUCKINGHAMSHIRE AND HERTFORDSHIRE:** Mick Payne.
Twenty rides on- and off-road for all the family.

**LEAFING THROUGH LITERATURE:
Writers' Lives in Hertfordshire and Bedfordshire**: David Carroll.
Illustrated short biographies of many famous authors and their
connections with these counties.

THROUGH VISITORS' EYES: A Bedfordshire Anthology:
edited by Simon Houfe.
Impressions of the county by famous visitors over the last four
centuries, thematically arranged and illustrated with line drawings.

**THE HILL OF THE MARTYR:
An Architectural History of St. Albans Abbey**: Eileen Roberts.
Scholarly and readable chronological narrative history of
Hertfordshire and Bedfordshire's famous cathedral. Fully illustrated
with photographs and plans.

LOCAL WALKS: South Bedfordshire and North Chilterns:
Vaughan Basham. Twenty-seven thematic circular walks.

LOCAL WALKS : North and Mid-Bedfordshire: Vaughan Basham.
Twenty-five thematic circular walks.

**CHILTERN WALKS: Hertfordshire, Bedfordshire and
North Buckinghamshire**: Nick Moon.

CHILTERN WALKS: Buckinghamshire: Nick Moon.

CHILTERN WALKS: Oxfordshire and West Buckinghamshire:
Nick Moon. A trilogy of circular walks, in association with the
Chiltern Society. Each volume contains thirty circular walks.

**OXFORDSHIRE WALKS: Oxford, the Cotswolds and
the Cherwell Valley**: Nick Moon.

**OXFORDSHIRE WALKS: Oxford, the Downs and
the Thames Valley:** Nick Moon.
Two volumes that complement Chiltern Walks: Oxfordshire and
complete coverage of the county, in association with the Oxford
Fieldpaths Society. Thirty circular walks in each.

**FOLK: Characters and Events in the History of Bedfordshire and
Northamptonshire**: Vivienne Evans. Anthology about people of
yesteryear – arranged alphabetically by village or town.

LEGACIES: Tales and Legends of Luton and the North Chilterns:
Vic Lea. Twenty-five mysteries and stories based on fact, including Luton Town Football Club. Many photographs.

ECHOES: Tales And Legends of Bedfordshire and Hertfordshire:
Vic Lea. Thirty, compulsively retold historical incidents.

MYTHS and WITCHES, PEOPLE and POLITICS:
Tales from Four Shires: Bucks., Beds., Herts., and Northants.:
John Houghton.
Anthology of strange but true historical events.

ECCENTRICS and VILLAINS, HAUNTINGS and HEROES.:
Tales from Four Shires: Northants., Beds., Bucks. and Herts.:
John Houghton.
True incidents and curious events covering one thousand years.

THE RAILWAY AGE IN BEDFORDSHIRE: Fred Cockman.
Classic, illustrated account of early railway history.

JOHN BUNYAN: HIS LIFE AND TIMES: Vivienne Evans.
Foreword by the Bishop of Bedford. Preface by Terry Waite.
Bedfordshire's most famous son set in his seventeenth century context.

SWANS IN MY KITCHEN: The Story of a Swan Sanctuary:
Lis Dorer. Foreword by Dr Philip Burton. Updated edition.
Tales of her dedication to the survival of these beautiful birds through her sanctuary near Hemel Hempstead.

WHIPSNADE WILD ANIMAL PARK: 'MY AFRICA': Lucy Pendar.
Foreword by Andrew Forbes. Introduction by Gerald Durrell.
Inside story of sixty years of the Park's animals and people – full of anecdotes, photographs and drawings.

DUNSTABLE WITH THE PRIORY, 1100–1550: Vivienne Evans.
Dramatic growth of Henry I's important new town around a major crossroads.

DUNSTABLE DECADE: THE EIGHTIES: –
A Collection of Photographs: Pat Lovering.
A souvenir book of nearly 300 pictures of people and events in the 1980s.

DUNSTABLE IN DETAIL: Nigel Benson.
A hundred of the town's buildings and features, plus town trail map.

OLD DUNSTABLE: Bill Twaddle.
A new edition of this collection of early photographs.

BOURNE AND BRED: A Dunstable Boyhood Between the Wars:
Colin Bourne.
An elegantly written, well-illustrated book capturing the spirit of the town over fifty years ago.

ROYAL HOUGHTON: Pat Lovering.
Illustrated history of Houghton Regis from the earliest times to the present.

**BEDFORDSHIRE'S YESTERYEARS Vol. 1: The Family,
Childhood and Schooldays:** Brenda Fraser-Newstead.
Unusual early 20th century reminiscences, with private photographs.

BEDFORDSHIRE'S YESTERYEARS Vol 2: The Rural Scene:
Brenda Fraser-Newstead.
Vivid first-hand accounts of country life two or three generations ago.

THE CHANGING FACE OF LUTON: An Illustrated History:
Stephen Bunker, Robin Holgate and Marian Nichols.
Luton's development from earliest times to the present busy
industrial town. Illustrated in colour and monochrome. The three
authors from Luton Museum are all experts in local history,
archaeology, crafts and social history.

**THE MEN WHO WORE STRAW HELMETS:
Policing Luton, 1840–1974:** Tom Madigan.
Meticulously chronicled history; dozens of rare photographs; author
served Luton Police for nearly fifty years.

BETWEEN THE HILLS: The Story of Lilley, a Chiltern Village:
Roy Pinnock.
A priceless piece of our heritage – the rural beauty remains but the
customs and way of life described here have largely disappeared.

FARM OF MY CHILDHOOD, 1925–1947: Mary Roberts.
An almost vanished lifestyle on a remote farm near Flitwick.

**THE TALL HITCHIN SERGEANT:
A Victorian Crime Novel based on fact:** Edgar Newman.
Mixes real police officers and authentic background with an exciting
storyline.

SPECIALLY FOR CHILDREN

VILLA BELOW THE KNOLLS: A Story of Roman Britain:
Michael Dundrow.
An exciting adventure for young John in Totternhoe and Dunstable
two thousand years ago.

ADVENTURE ON THE KNOLLS: A Story of Iron Age Britain:
Michael Dundrow.
Excitement on Totternhoe Knolls as ten-year-old John finds himself
back in those dangerous times, confronting Julius Caesar and his army.

THE RAVENS: One Boy Against the Might of Rome: James Dyer.
On the Barton Hills and in the south-east of England as the men of
the great fort of Ravensburgh (near Hexton) confront the invaders.

Further titles are in preparation.
All the above are available via any bookshop, or from the
publisher and bookseller

**THE BOOK CASTLE
12 Church Street, Dunstable, Bedfordshire, LU5 4RU
Tel: (01582) 605670**